RAINBOWS & WINDMILLS

ABOUT THE AUTHOR

PETER TARLETON STEWART has acted as a chaplain in schools, prisons, hospitals and a university. He also has worked as a parish clergyman in Cork, Dublin, Cootehill, Killeshin and Portlaise, retiring in 2020 after 46 years as an Anglican priest. He has always been actively interested in politics, recognising how it often serves the interests of the few to the exclusion of the most vulnerable. As a Christian he sees the world as a place in which to be actively involved. He has called on the church to be bold in its service to humanity, and respectful in its care of the Earth.

RAINBOWS
&
WINDMILLS

21st Century Spirituality

PETER TARLETON STEWART

columba
BOOKS

First published in 2022 by

 columbaBOOKS

Block 3b, Bracken Business Park,
Bracken Road, Sandyford,Dublin 18, D18 K277
www.columbabooks.com

ISBN: 978-1-78218-390-7

Set in Freight Text Pro and Freight Sans Pro 11.5/15.5
Cover and book design by Alba Esteban | Columba Books

Printed by L&C, Poland.

I dedicate this modest contribution to
the development of
person-centred Spirituality
to my children

Joanne Marie
Catherine Ann
Michael Peter
Eoin Denis
Kevin David Thomas

with much delight and appreciation
for seeing me through tough times
and for all you have taught me.

Contents

Preface

BY REV MIKE DIXON

The contemporary discourse about religion frequently concludes with something like, "I'm not really religious, but I AM spiritual." This often then develops into an apologia for religion and a discussion about the relationship between spirituality and religion. Peter Tarleton faces this seeming dichotomy head-on.

In this book, Peter accepts the reality of a person-centred spirituality. He builds on it as a real and crucial grown-up element in human experience. He does not set spirituality over against faith or religion, but rather embraces personal spirituality and illustrates its reality, employing his own journey through life, a journey that draws on his rich and deep encounters and experiences.

Read the tales from his:

- Irish Protestant upbringing,
- Parish life,
- Theological studies,
- University Chaplaincy,
- Prison Chaplaincy,
- Hospital Chaplaincy,
- Psychoanalysis,
- Multi-faith dialogues

and the ordinary life struggles with faith, healing and relationships that we all encounter. This is a truly incarnational spirituality.

The book is full of challenges:

- challenges for a moribund, irrelevant establishment church,
- challenges for secular institutions in their various forms,
- challenges to fundamentalists of all faiths and none,
- challenges for individuals (including himself) to face up to who we are and where we are going.

This book is not without hope. Various tools are offered, some traditional, some current and imaginative, to assess where we are and how we might develop and continue the exploration of our own journey of faith.

The "Negative Design Criteria", from Ivan D Illich's work, seems particularly relevant in today's world, in the ways both the secular and faith systems organise themselves. The model is:

- Idealism
- then Institutionalisation
- Decline
- and Corruption.

This seems an appropriate description of the current dysfunction of the British Labour Party? And one must ask where faith communities are in the process of this circle? It must be asked whether the circle can be broken. Was the circle broken in the past by the likes of St Francis or John Wesley? Can the initial idealism be restored? Or will we discover a new idealism for our present age?

This book raises many questions. Peter comes from a particular Northern Irish Protestant tradition. One would like a response from the Catholic spiritual tradition, or indeed from a Jewish rabbi, or a Moslem imam. But regardless of the origins of our faith, questioning is a key part of a person-centred spirituality.

Why "Windmills and Rainbows"? Because each of these physical entities carries with it many familiar images, stories, allegories, signs and symbols about power and light – providing a framework in which to explore spirituality.

If you are interested in how the spiritual journey can mesh into your personal history through the maze of existence, then reading this book, and meditating on its contents, will enhance your understanding.

....

Rev Mike Dixon is an Anglican priest, ordained in 1966. He was a curate in Durham and Yorkshire before becoming a full-time Prison Chaplain, where he served in Liverpool, Onley, Frankland (top security), Durham (including the women's wing) and Acklington. He continued as a priest in rural Northumberland, and, following his retirement, was elected as Labour Councillor to Durham County Council, including a year as Vice Chairman. On further retirement, he now helps out in the Diocese of Durham and produces a Jazz Programme for Aycliffe Radio.

Introduction

Spirituality, as I understand it, is expressed both as a personal dimension *and* as community – but not necessarily both at the same time. Person-centred spirituality is often seen by faith leaders as an "out" for people from the faith community, subsequently reducing their power and control of the religious agenda. It is regarded as a "me-me-me" sort of distraction from the centrality of God in all things religious. To ask questions, or dismiss unhelpful baggage from the Christian inheritance, is to undermine the presumed integrity of the faith.

Well, start asking now:

"What is a faith which needs unquestioning obedience in reality?"

It is a place of absolute certainty, which
requires *no faith* at all.

Faith becomes visible through searching and "explory".[1] Faith that falters and missteps has an inherent authenticity. When the community scapegoats the enquirer – the seeker – it closes another door to the light and the truth it claims to profess and seek out. If my spirit rejoices – or collapses – in the present, is that not at least as important as the experience of someone in the past? Must we refer everything back to a past third-party historical experience and so deny our present reality?

I believe Christian communities are ill-equipped to encourage and celebrate contemporary experience. Even when people do have ecstatic tales to report, they are usually viewed through the prism of an experience of some biblical person, defined by the church. This diminishes the person *and* the reality of the spiritual experience. It unhelpfully glorifies the past.

Could it be that a kindly smile on the face of a stranger at the bus stop might light up your day in much the same way that Saul encountered that bright light on the road to Damascus? Yes, I know Paul was blinded by the experience and that he claimed to hear Jesus' voice at the same time. It was overwhelming, and the subsequent meeting in Antioch added something significant to the story. Please, just allow me to set wider parameters for experiencing and understanding spiritual reality.

I am the subject of *this* story. You are the subject of *yours*. We may compare our experiences and understanding, but even when everything appears comparable, we are still two very different people. Much of our childhood faith developed around the stories we heard, and we understood them solely in the context of our own lives. What the teachers of these stories failed to do was to help us *grow* those insights and wisdom into an adult faith that can be credible in the real world.

Much of our Christian spirituality is childish. It projects our goodness onto God, thereby denying the possibility of our innate personal goodness. It projects our misbehaviour onto the devil, thereby missing out on the opportunity to acknowledge our human weakness and uncover the forgiveness and healing which lie at the heart of our faith.

These thoughts began in my childhood and came to be formulated while I was a parent, with my wife Joss, to five wonderful children. Some of the content of the following pages was gathered while leading school assemblies for Wigan Deanery High in the mid-eighties. The colour of Rainbow and the power of Windmill were truth for young people. There is no denying beauty and science, as young people discern meaning in the world around them.

Relatively recently, I discovered that I had spent most of my life "growing up". Much of my childhood was privileged – I am a white Anglo-Saxon male. I imagined myself to be someone special, while being deprived of affirmation and encouragement. So, for many later years, I spent hours with psychotherapists (one at a time!) trying to unravel the distress which accompanied my development. I thank those therapists for their attention, for which I paid only the going rate. There *are* compensations around an overlong childhood – among them, never losing a sense of fun and spontaneity.

I want to acknowledge the generous patience of all those people who entered the orbit of my life, and who allowed me to enter theirs, during these years of emotional dysfunction. I am vain enough, still, to imagine that I have grown "up" because of my optimism and endurance. Yet I completely appreciate the great tolerance and forbearance shown to me by so many people throughout my life, so far. You have been my teachers and spiritual guides – I owe you.

I was born into a travelling clergy family, headed by a serious priest. My father, Denis, was anxious that I would not believe myself to be "too clever". When I was twelve, he sent me to a boarding school where several teachers who had taught him as a boy were happy to confirm to me that I was "not half the student" that my father was. I ran away frequently from that setting.

I tell you this to explain how the origins of my personal spirituality grew out of a well of disapproval and an incomparable sense of shortcoming. Only later in my life did I learn that my dad's childhood had been the endurance of such disapproval, too. He taught me what he had learned, and without diminishing his paternal strengths, he taught me well. Albeit, what I learned led me in the opposite direction. My own children will no doubt have experienced many forms of distress from having the father that I am. Check out "This be the Verse" by poet Philip Larkin.

A key component of spirituality is *living* – it is an "alive" thing! By implication, it is growing, it is moving, it has energy – and it is real and present. When you put it like that, it seems to leave religion a long way behind! So much of religion, as we know it, is past, repetitive, stifling and exhausted. Why would we want to have anything to do with that? It is not for me to evaluate your faith tradition for you. I can only observe and comment. You decide how you continue a relationship with your religious community, *and on whose terms.*

Well, when we have looked at the essential elements of a vibrant spirituality, then we can decide if there is a religion out there that can accommodate, and even assist with, our spiritual development. Do not ask, "Am I good enough for my religion?" but, "Is my religion good enough for me?" We shall come to that in Chapter 2 when you can see how this entire issue of spiritual reality begins with you and moves out from there.

Having become a Quaker in 1990 (as well as an Anglican) I discovered the beauty and power of silence in community. Over the years, I had attended retreats in monasteries where common breakfast was often shared in total silence – well, not so much silence as unspoken words. Visitors could sometimes sense the unexpressed tensions between the brothers. I am sure it would have been much healthier if, like children, they had just screamed their distress across the room at each other!

In the Quaker world, to worship in silence – to feel the strength of the presence of Friends around you – was a real awakening to the inner workings of spirit. One of the key tenets of the Society of Friends (Quakers) is to "recognise that of God in everyone"; to see the divine in every human being. This is a serious challenge within the Quaker community, let alone applying it to the wider world.

I have two good reasons for publishing this book now.

First, there is an unhealthy tsunami of Christian fundamentalism claiming to be *the* voice of the church in the world today. What they are offering to people facing the challenges of the present time is an ancient God of disapproval and judgement. This is a "Youse are all damned"[2] message – implying that somehow the world is getting what it deserves. You did not believe the Sodom and Gomorrah story (where God wiped out the entire population of the two cities because of their waywardness), so here is your own version! Their approach appears to be an invitation to lead people away from the *real* world, to avoid the notional punishment that will surely befall the rest of us. It is as though humanity is divisible in some arbitrary fashion between good people and bad people. However, what they are offering is simply not sufficient to satisfy the deeper needs of people.

The idea of holding up my hand and saying "yes" to the invitation to accept Jesus as Lord is merely a simplistic way to avoid taking responsibility for who I am and what I do. It separates me from parts of myself. I am invited into denial about my integrity as a human being. This is psychologically damaging to human beings. While there may be an initial surge of well-being when welcomed into this cheering fellowship, there is also an implied, unquestioning acceptance of all that the community believes.

When we have a question about why God allows bad things to happen, we are told that it is a test for us, or it is a mystery. No one says, "We don't *know*". So adult Christians are expected to put aside their capacity for reason. They must then collude with religious professionals who tell them that blind belief in Jesus will "save" them, or that their daring questions are from the devil. What nonsense.

Alongside this is a Biblical literalism that encourages Creationism, in conflict with our current understanding of science. This is dangerous because it causes confuses among children (and many adults too) unnecessarily around the learning of science. It limits their ability to resolve for themselves the tensions between science and faith.

Blind belief in the accuracy of the Bible is unwise. It is *not* an unerring document of God's words to his people. The Bible, and other holy books, do not have sufficient power and truth to meet the spiritual needs of humanity, regardless of what religious institutions may proclaim. Those writings come from their own time, and their message is not universal.

The wacky notion that the Earth is only just over 6,000 years old is implausible at best and downright deceptive at worst. You don't have to believe that Darwin has all the answers to our origins, but his theory of evolution deserves a *rational* response at the very least. In refusing to accept that we may have descended from the same evolutionary line as apes, we now behave like mind-less beings, with lower intelligence than many other creatures on the planet.

The message of simply trusting in Jesus and that will carry you through is ingrained into generations of Christians. This baseline is far from spiritual; it is cultic conditioning. It fails to meet most of our actual needs when life is *happening*. And then, there's the delusion that my endurance of suffering in *this* world will uncover glorious rewards in the next. Is that sufficient to help my struggle with relationships and my issues of self-esteem in the here and now? No. It simply leaves me feeling powerless in my own life.

Do you remember the story of a deeply Christian man who fell off a cliff, broke his back and legs, and when the lifeboat arrived he sent them away saying: "No, I am a man of prayer and the Lord has promised to save me!" And when the helicopter lowered a team with a stretcher to collect him, again he responded: "No, I'm a Christian and the Lord will save me!" He died. On arriving at heaven's gate, he was exasperated with the Almighty, demanding to know why he hadn't been "saved". God's response was: "I sent you the lifeboat and the helicopter. What more did you expect?" Maybe our sense of the spiritual needs to be prompted by what we encounter in the real world – rather than in our religious imaginings.

Second, I am 75 years old, and I see little optimism or encouragement in most expressions of the Christian faith in the world. I will die in the coming days, weeks or years and I will meet my end in how best suits my spirit – maybe screaming that I'm not yet ready to go, or sitting quietly and opening my arms to welcome what awaits me. My faith community preaches some kind of glory which could conceivably be mine *if* I say the right words to qualify, or claim to believe the incredible.

We will look at this "end-of-life" issue in a later chapter, but I mention it here because, in this respect, I have found no particular advantage in being a member of a Christian church. There is very little dynamic; little inspiration, imagination or flair; no meeting me at the point of my need. When the final moment comes, I know no one will step in there on my behalf. It will be *my* moment, my opportunity to discover what happens next. Whatever follows my death will come as a surprise – but then, we do like surprises!

Of course, there are inspiring verses in the Bible, particularly in some of the Psalms, which can help "carry" us through times of crisis. There are some inspiring verses from letters in the New Testament. And there is much excellent poetry elsewhere, in other literature, to heighten our sensitivity to a greater reality. However, standing to attention and reciting a series of dogmatic credal statements, which include a belief in "the resurrection of the dead", does not exactly give me a warm reassurance of divine continuity. Neither does the threat of eternal damnation curtail the liberation of my spirit.

To re-jig our awareness, and to re-frame our expectations and hopes, are processes necessary for the development of a lively human spirit. It is an exercise in divine growth from within. If, as my atheist friends assure me, "we are going no-where", then it is incumbent to "eat, drink and be merry!" And if we have confidence that there *is* a divine "future" in higher and deeper realms than we have yet experienced, it is still incumbent upon us to make the very most of our human existence – to live our lives to the max, here and now.

In this spirit of abounding Blessing, I choose to promote a *person*-centred spirituality, which recognises where we are as a human race, in challenge, crisis and opportunity. If we have found the capacity to recognise God in the people we meet – as Quakers try to do – then it is just as vital that we grow to identify and acknowledge that divinity within *ourselves*.

ENDNOTES

1. "Explory" – this is a word I like to use as an alternative to exploration or enquiry. Please indulge me in my petty linguistic creativity!

2. "Youse are all damned" is an expression of Ulster Protestant evangelical judgement which presumes the high moral ground, allowing the speaker to write off anyone who disagrees. ("Youse" = plural of you.)

—

CHAPTER 1

Childhood Experiences

I was afraid of the wind

When I was in a pushchair, taken out for a walk after lunch to get me to sleep, a wind might arise and create a sinister whistling sound through the telegraph wires. The sound haunted me. I cried – for no apparent reason. Maybe only 5 years old, my crying was dismissed by the accompanying adult – "Don't be silly! There is nothing to be afraid of." By the time I was 7, I had worked it all out with a little help and advice from my friends. I grew to like the sound, the energy of something I could not see. I wasn't silly – I was and am in awe of the wind.

I was afraid of the water

One summer, when I was 7 years old, we were on holiday near Portstewart where there were bathing pools built onto the rocks. They were about 4 feet deep and big enough to accommodate an inflatable dinghy. I was "boarding" a dinghy when it somehow bumped away from the edge and I fell down the gap. As I floated up, I was trapped by the bottom of the dinghy. Terrified, I panicked and screamed, swallowing lots of water. It seemed to me like an eternity, though in reality it was only a couple of minutes before I was pulled out of the pool. I retched up a lot of salt water, followed by whatever I had eaten for lunch. When I had recovered a little, I was offered another chance to get into the dinghy. I just cried until someone brought me back to our holiday home.

I was afraid of the dark

On Tuesday and Thursday evenings I had to leave the badminton club early, to be in bed by 9.30 pm. So I walked home in the dark – alone. I rushed past the graveyard on the side of the road the footpath was on, with only an uncertain "jungle" of briars and trees behind the opposite hedge. I whistled as I ran, hoping to banish visions of "the resurrection of the dead" from my 10-year-old imagination. I knew it was silly, but my head was full of all those religious horror images of hell and damnation.

If you were distracted by such thoughts, my mother would have analysed it as a sign of a "bad conscience". Despite an outward appearance of goodness, I knew by then that I was a poor specimen of humanity. How could a child ever conjure up such self-deprecation? I consoled myself with the fact that I knew some children who were even worse than I was! Yet, my good fortune in life has been to encounter a host of people who exuded the warmth of human love and encouragement, people who would always help get me through to the light.

The Garden

At the end of the village, close to the Gospel Hall, there was a garden encircled by a long stone wall with broken glass on top to deter access. The door of blistered blue paint closed tight at a slight angle against a rotting frame, with a bolt and a lock – uninviting, to say the least. One day, at the invitation of the owner, my mum and I found the door slightly ajar, so we pushed it open and walked right in. There we discovered an amazing, beautifully ordered place. Neat weedless pathways and immaculate flower beds were bursting with beautiful blooms, offering an overwhelming range of powerful fragrances.

A yew tree (Life/Death) and a monkey puzzle tree (Knowledge) tree were at opposite ends of the garden. Birds, butterflies and bees abounded in this setting. It was rich with sensual delights. I experienced a stimulating awareness of something wonderful – even beyond hearing, sight or smell. From that July sunshine of 1952 was born a memory to burnish much of the desolation and despair that would cast a shadow over my life in the years that followed. In an early school class two months later, our teacher read a creation story from Genesis. When the Garden of Eden was mentioned, I nudged Jim Stevenson, who was sitting beside me, and whispered: "I know where that is. I've been there!"

Part of my earliest learning was that children belonged to the Kingdom – where we might expect to see lovely flowers, friendly faces and sense sweet smells – "All things bright and beautiful". At the beach, I would engineer tidy roadways in the sand, with cars and lorries parked in rows – my neat little ordered universe, where I was in charge. But, inevitably, someone would walk all over my "world", or the tide would come in and wash it all away. My designs on life were doomed only to be temporary.

Whatever delights that little oasis of childhood created in me, adults soon "got" to me. Slowly, I realised not everyone was *in*. This kingdom is for me only if I'm good and if I'm careful – certainly not for "others" who do not belong. Many adults so often said NO. Heaven is for the "good". I gave up expecting heaven; this child was just too bad, too often.

Some teachers felt it their duty to inflict punishment by the use of a cane. One female teacher, in a fit of bad temper, cut open my ear with her cane because she "found" me whispering to the boy beside me. My bad temper was roused sufficiently to grab the stick from her, break it in two, and then four, and throw it into the fire behind her desk. Later, when my father found out about the incident, he punched me in the other ear.

Another teacher refused to let me go to the toilet during class. After 10 minutes, I could not hold it in any longer and I peed all over the floor. I felt so ashamed and went red in the face. There was nothing I could do. The laughter of the other children drew the teacher's attention, and she also made fun of me. I can recall trying to convince the girls on the bus home that I had somehow slipped into a puddle after school, but they knew I had pissed myself.

The child heard: the poor, the broken, the sad and lonely, the sick, the grieving – theirs is the Kingdom.

The child heard: NO, as in "No, you may not", NO, as in "NO Surrender", or "NO Pope here", not as expressions of love, nor identification with the poor or broken – rather an emphatic disapproval of the celebration of the essence of life.

The child heard: faith as a cry of fear – sometimes of emptiness. The invitation to belong had a hollowness to it, a bitterness that reminded me of Mr Strong's bad breath (more about that later).

Somewhere, too, the child heard: "Love your enemies" – love the bad people. I remember once asking my father how we might love our Roman Catholic "enemies"? Without hesitation, he told me we must just love our Protestant enemies. So, I began to undermine this by loving Catholics, and thereby unwittingly discovered Protestant enemies!

The first of these was Miss Buchanan, who used to mind us when our parents were out for the evening. She was related to the bishop and had observed my "behaviour" around the village for several years. One night, when I was supposed to be asleep upstairs, I heard my dad and Miss B talking in the hallway below. They were discussing *me*, and that was when, at Miss B's direction, the decision was made to send me away to boarding school – "in everyone's best interests"!

At that same boarding school, one night around 12.30, our House Master woke up all the boys in our dorm. His bedroom was next door to the dorm. He had come in loudly, under the influence of alcohol. The usual whispered remarks were made around the ten of us. Then the door was pushed open, and the light switched on. He claimed to have heard some noise from us and asked, "Who?"

When no one owned up, he called all of us downstairs to line up outside his study for a caning. He raised my dressing gown and struck me until blood appeared on my pyjama bottoms. I understood that some of the other boys experienced the same degree of abuse. My father would not believe it when I told him; he would not even let me show him the welts. By the end of that school year, I was allowed home to attend the nearest secondary day school.

This experience might have been in other people's best interests, but certainly not in mine. If I were to survive in this confusion, then I really had to start making up my own rules.

Aughadarragh (*Oak Grove*)

Aughadarragh is a townland in County Tyrone. For this young boy, it was where the Biblical events of Crucifixion, Resurrection and Burning Bush are all located. It is also the townland in which the Weir family lived.

In the mid-1950s, I often walked the mile and a half out to Weir's to spend a Sunday afternoon "helping" to look after their animals, chatting with Mr & Mrs Weir and their sons

Jim and John. More than once I was hoisted onto the back of their donkey, and, just as often, I was unceremoniously thrown onto my backside on the ground!

It was Sunday the 4th of November 1956, and we were listening to the BBC Radio News. There was an announcement that the Russians had invaded Hungary to check a rebellion, which had taken place there over several months. This was a frightening development in the Cold War and a reminder that, for many people, freedom did not exist as it did for us. I imagined I felt the seriousness with which the adults in the room were hearing this momentous news.

When I got home that evening, my parents were talking about the possibility of "adopting" one of the Hungarian refugees who, it was anticipated, would be displaced over the coming weeks. We never did. Instead, a Miss Davis arrived, an elderly cousin of one of our parishioners who needed a "retirement" home. There was lots of space in our rectory, so she was welcomed for the duration. She never became an "enemy" as such, but one of her basic premises was that children should "be seen, but not heard", and frequently complained to my mother that we children were a disturbance. Usually, that was my fault – even when it wasn't!

But, back to Mrs Jemima Weir, who always made sure that there was bread and scones, and butter and jam, available in her home for family and visitors. She baked lovely currant buns and soda bread, which never lasted long! But what impressed me most about her was being in the presence of a woman whose joints were distorted by severe arthritis, yet she never uttered a word of complaint – expressing concern only for people less fortunate than herself.

She worked tirelessly for her family and on one day every week, usually Saturday morning, she walked into the village to do her shopping. She would then walk back home, laden with a heavy bag in each hand. She often refused a lift from passing cars, except in the worst of weather. And if I walked with her sometimes, she would not accept any offer of help in carrying her bags. Despite her visible frailty, she showed her great strength, determination and perseverance, even as her fingers grew ever more gnarled by her arthritis.

Some 15 years later, when being interviewed for ordination training, I was asked who might have set me off on "the road to religion". I told the enquirer: "Mrs Weir". He knew that I had grown up in a clergy home and that in my travels I had encountered some "interesting" people, including bishops, so he thought I was joking about Mrs Weir. I certainly was not. This lady was a truly wonderful spiritual leader, displaying nothing more than her quiet willingness to love and to endure.

Of course, he had never met her – he had not walked home with her from the village, nor listened to her words of encouragement and hope; he had not witnessed the delight she took in her two teenage boys, Jim and John; the brightness her smile brought to a room; the pride she took in her whole family and her willingness to work for the good of our church community. By any standards, Jemima was a model of divine living. She generated a sense of spiritual wonder in what she did, in the place where she lived, and in the person she was.

The crucifixion took place on a rise about 100 yards from her front door – and the resurrection in a rocky face, on the other side of the hill. The burning bush was further away in a field, which had a few hawthorns along one hedge. Did Jemima make these images real for me, or did I just apply the remembered story to locations of my own experience? I guess it was a bit of both.

Mr Strong's Visit

Every Sunday afternoon my older sister Rosemary and I used to go to an evangelistic Sunday School. I remember the enthusiastic singing of choruses, the flannel-graph pictures accompanying Bible stories, and the bright stamps which we were given each week to stick onto our attendance cards. I never actively looked forward to these meetings, nor did I refuse to attend – even though by lunchtime I had already spent an hour in another Sunday School and an hour at a church service.

Then, on one "special" Sunday, we were visited by Mr Strong – a Gospel Hall leader from another village. He was dressed in a pin-striped suit, with which he wore wellington boots. His cheeks were bright red. As we lined up to sing the first chorus, our names were attached to our tops with a pin. The song went something like this: "We've been washed, we've been washed, we've been washed in the blood of the lamb..."

When it ended, our visitor came to me, being the smallest, at one end of the line, leaned down into my face, exuding a foul-smelling breath, and asked: "Well, Peter, have you been washed in the blood of the lamb?" I felt myself going very hot and tears welled up within me. I burst into a wail, ran out the door and did not stop running until I got back to the house nearly 15 minutes later.

I already disliked blood, and I was a complete coward around needles, cuts and injuries. Never would I – or could I – become a doctor. Even singing that chorus earlier, I had never pictured real red blood, not until Mr Strong spelt it out! The imagery of his question made me aware of something very distasteful in this religion. I avoided having to attend that Sunday afternoon experience ever again. No questions were asked! I was 7 at the time.

The Milkman

Fergus drove a VW van as though it were a racing car, with crates rattling like a steel band! When he was nearing the end of the "round", his raised spirits caused him to sing – as if he were holding a microphone in front of a crowd of fans. "Cherry pink and apple blossom white" featured regularly, and he added realistic trumpet sounds, which gave the impression of a star performance!

I worked so hard with him each Saturday, enjoying every minute of the experience, as well as getting a shilling pocket money. When life offers you such delight, there really is a sense of blessing. It could not last – Fergus was a Catholic! "Catholic" was a word which my dear grandfather, Robert Stewart, uttered *sotto voce* – as though it were a word that should never be heard out loud.

Now Robert was a Blackmouth Presbyterian.[3] His church disapproved of alcohol, cigarettes and playing cards (the devil's tools). Sunday dinner had to be prepared the day before so as not to "break the Sabbath" by working on the Lord's Day. However, my grandparents were "creative" in interpreting these rules. Granny Jeannie smoked like a chimney. Grampa loved an occasional sherry. They held whist and bridge parties at their home a couple of nights a week, and the Sunday papers were delivered to Harris's next door and passed over the back wall!

(Because of that benign guiding influence of my maternal grandparents, I have added their surname to that of my father's for the purpose of authoring this book.)

The Forge

There was a forge at the other end of the village, and if I broke anything metal I brought it to the blacksmith – though

I can't remember if I ever knew him by name. He shoed horses – which at that time had not yet been replaced by tractors in the mainly small-farm community. It was a great place to spend a few hours on a cold wintry day, gazing into the fire and taking turns to lean on the bellows to keep the blaze going. He made me metal runners for an old sleigh I had repaired, and it turned out to be the fastest I ever owned. Every time we passed this place, I asked my dad to toot the horn. He wouldn't because – you've guessed it! – he was another Catholic. Where did I find them all?

The Protestant Orphan Collection

When I was about 10 years old and still in primary school, I was invited along with others in the class to collect for the Protestant Orphan Society. We were given a card, and each person we approached had to write their name and the amount given, so there was no room for misappropriation! There was a prize of a 2lb bag of sweets for the person in our class who collected the most money. I was up early and out late – I even needed a second, and then a third card, to accommodate all the contacts I had made.

On the closing day, I had five pounds and one shilling. I remember going to the Ulster Bank the Friday before to exchange all but one of my coins for a big white Fiver – giving my collection some special dignity! The only other person who came anywhere near my total was a boy called Eric, who had collected exactly five pounds. I was thrilled at the prospect of winning the big bag of sweets.

BUT! During break that morning, while we were playing in the yard, the principal went through the respective collecting cards and detected that I had included two shillings donated by a Roman Catholic lady. When we returned to class, she told me off in front of the class and said that I would have to return the two shillings. From the bags of cash, she selected a Free State (Irish Republic) two-shilling piece, with a fish on one side, to be returned to the donor. Now Eric had won the prize because he had one shilling more than me. I felt my world crumbling, but I held it together, at least on the outside, until I could go to Mrs Connolly at lunchtime and return her donation.

As I walked up the path to her house, she opened the door and said, "Come on in, Peter. Is it about that money I gave you the other day?" Without saying a word, as soon as I entered the house I burst into tears. "I knew it," she said, as I sobbed out the story, "some people don't want there to be any mixing in this town". I had little idea what she meant. I did not know what the "problem" was. I had been welcomed into her home a few times before, as her son Kevin used to help me repair my bike when it was broken.

Mrs Connolly saved my day and recovered my spirits when she brought out two Spring-sprawn marshmallow biscuits and poured me a glass of brown lemonade. As I sniffed away the last of my sorrow, she returned the two-shilling piece into my hand and said "Well, Peter, you just keep that for yourself." It was like she had bounced me back up to the heights of expectation I'd felt earlier in the day.

Eric had indeed won the bag of sweets. I had won another, greater prize – and had learnt some useful lessons! I did not know that you could tell who was a Catholic by their surname, or by the height of their cheekbone! My education was developing.

Priceless Lemons available locally

One day when I was on my way home from school, I saw some lemons on the back of a fruit truck. Why should lemons attract my attention? Well, a couple of days earlier, my mother had asked me to buy two lemons, but none were available at the time. So, here they were, now I could fulfil the order, so I just helped myself. With a sense of achievement, five minutes later, I handed them over to mum as I entered the house. She was smiling and declared an OTT "Thank you. Where did you get these?" I had become quite adept at lying and assured her that I had just come across them. Her smile vanished: "You will go straight back down to McDermott's and apologise for *stealing* these lemons and pay for them out of your own pocket money". The electric telephone had undermined my criminal intent by giving my mother advance warning.

At the shop, the man behind the counter laughed at me as I came in: "You're the smart thief, Peter, lifting stuff while two of us were watching you through the winda!" He accepted the apology and the money, and then, to my surprise, asked me if I was free the next day, Saturday, as he was short of help in the store. Two shillings for a morning's work was a great incentive for a 10-year-old, with an occasional lemon gifted teasingly just to remind me of my offending past! I worked there on Saturdays for 8 or 9 weeks before an accident with the bacon-slicer ended that association.

A finger on my left hand needed serious stitching in Omagh General hospital. The result was a light cast on the injured finger, preventing me from doing my piano practice. This pleased me greatly and led to the end of piano instruction altogether. Later, in secondary school, I found I was much more suited to the French horn. Can you see the *karma* factor here? There are just penalties for making bad choices, and yet there can be rewards even within that process of justice.

Cycling Ban

Having a bicycle was a means of being free. I could get away from the village and spend time with the friends I chose to be with. At 11 years of age, the challenge of riding the bike without hands was fairly universal. But to ride without hands *and* feet required a long hill and a bit of skill and daring. A few miles out the Fintona Road there was just such a hill, near the home of a school friend, David. On this particular day, my friend was in front – hands-free – and as I followed, at speed, I managed to get my feet on the handlebars, and roared a "Yippee!" David looked round to see, and at that moment a van came round the corner and stopped dead. His bike hit the front and he flew over it, landing head-first on the road.

The result was a fractured skull for David and a very sorry ending to such unauthorised trials. About a week later, I was in the kitchen and could see the RUC Sergeant Glenny pushing his bike up the drive. I hid under the table and hoped that he would not take me away. Following a lengthy conversation with the sergeant at the front door, my mother came back to inform me that I was not allowed to ride the bicycle for the next 6 months, nor was I welcome to play with my friend again. I was just relieved not to have been arrested and locked up. After 2 months, the sergeant got a transfer to another area, and my ban sort of "lapsed".

Miss Buchanan was in high dudgeon! Mind you, as I look back, she had a point. All this behaviour was probably reflecting badly on my father's work in the community. That was perhaps a karma issue for him too, but since neither of us was aware of it at the time, that underlying truth did not surface.

Car accident

At the end of May 1956, when I was just 9, I was allowed a Friday off school to go with my dad to the Balmoral Show in Lisburn or Belfast. I was often sick on car journeys. My mother smoked, but no one made the connection between passive smoking and carsickness. However, on this day I could sit in the front where I knew I never got sick. I was half-turned towards my father for much of the trip, chatting away excitedly about what lay ahead.

I have no memory of the crash at all. I woke up three days later in Portadown Hospital, feeling groggy and hungry. My first meal did not go down so well, in that it came straight back up again! My dad was still in intensive care, with broken ribs and breathing problems. On impact with the lorry, most of my body had gone through the windscreen. My throat had been cut deeply, with additional injuries to my forehead and leg. Apparently, things looked bleak for me in the early stages, but by day five I was helping the nurses hand out the meals to the other patients. I went home after seven days. My father followed two days later.

I had no idea of the fragile nature of the human condition. My recovery suggested a normal capacity for the body to get it together, even after such massive trauma. As I had not seen the crash coming, I had no nightmares, nor fear of getting into a car subsequently. My father had been hospitalised several times earlier in my life. I saw no reason then to perceive an automatic association between hospital and the end of life. I do not remember being treated any differently when I got back home, and when other children asked, I let them touch the fragments of the triplex glass still inside the skin under my chin after the operation. Around the year 2000, one of these "bits" surfaced as a reminder. The last piece remains and is a slight nuisance when shaving.

* * *

It is worth mentioning at this stage that at the end of August 1957, Sergeant Arthur Ovens of the RUC was killed in an IRA booby trap bomb at a cottage near Coalisland, County Tyrone. Arthur was a first cousin of my father. Little was spoken about this in our home, but it underlined some of the suspicions that our family had towards the Nationalist community – and their subsequent horror at my involvement with the Civil Rights activity in Derry 12 years later.

Our God was a White Anglo-Saxon Protestant (WASP) who used the Union Jack to brighten up his creation! The tenets of the Orange Order[4], while affirming Protestantism and the importance of the Bible, were basically anti-Roman Catholic. The entire Protestant community at that time was anti-Irish and anti-Republican. Essentially, we were anti-everything! Yet somehow, by the mid-1960s, our straitjacket had loosened just a little, and we dared to visit Dublin to watch international rugby matches.

They held the Twelfth of July celebrations in our village one year. I believe it was in 1956. By 1 o'clock that day, I had my fill of bands and drums. I took my headache home and went to bed, unable to sleep for the throbbing sounds of the drums even from far away. In other years, I was brought to the "Twelfth Field", where Orange leaders and politicians gave speeches. It was all very predictable for a boy who had heard the word "No" sufficiently often to find it dry and empty, like a well where the water had run out.

To be a member of the Protestant community was like being a supporter of one of the opposing local football teams, which raised a certain passion and identity. Maybe the Twelfth of July was the pinnacle of that emotion for many (but not for me!). Orangeism wrapped the whole faith/spirituality issue in with cultural patterns, so they could be perceived as one. As children in Sunday School, we were given a little pamphlet: "How we differ from Rome" – a helpful guide to nurturing sectarianism. This was Anti-testant in that it appeared necessary to denigrate the opposition's beliefs before expressing our own.

The same Orange Lodge included the shop floor worker and the businessman or landowner as members together. The underlying idea appeared to be to prevent Protestant workers from realising that they had more in common with Catholic workers and every reason to be sceptical about the agenda of the wealthy landowners.

However, several decades later, as families attended funerals in each other's churches, they realised how much we had in common with Roman Catholics. The change of worship language from Latin to English in the Catholic tradition made this very obvious. Now it was clear that there was much less to divide us, to separate us, to make us enemies. Still, for many, it mattered little.

In January 1982, my young family moved with me to Cootehill, County Cavan. One evening as I followed a funeral down to the Roman Catholic Church, holding my son Eoin's hand, we went with the crowd towards the church door. "We don't go in, your Reverence," a voice said into my ear. "Oh, don't you, Johnny," I replied, and walked straight in. The next day at the funeral Mass, several other Protestants dared to join me entering the church to pay their respects to the deceased. The times they were a-changing, but slowly. Another "No" had been prompted in my direction, but by now I had found an appropriate response. No need to argue, just do what you feel is right.

> "It is in changing that things find repose."
> – HERACLITUS

ENDNOTES

3. *Black Mouth Presbyterians.* Church of Ireland people (Anglicans) used this as a nickname, to remind the Presbyterians that you could tell them by the black colouring around their mouth from eating blackberries while attending illegal secret worship behind hedges outside town.

4. *Orange Order.* Orange Institution of Ireland (*says of itself*) "This is exclusively a Protestant Association; yet detesting an intolerant spirit, it admits no persons into its brotherhood who are not well known to be incapable of persecuting, injuring or upbraiding anyone on account of his religious opinion: its principle is, to aid and assist loyal subjects of every religious persuasion, by protecting them from violence and oppression."

CHAPTER 2

—

Essential Elements of Spirituality

When spirituality is so closely identified with religion, it is difficult to pick out its distinctive nature. It feels as though it is a holy entity, bigger than we are, and has no access for personal input. As we compare and contrast the elements of this subject, let's remember that this process is for clarification, and not to indicate preference for one over the other. Spirituality can abound within a good religion; good spirituality will enhance a religion's effectiveness.

Spirit is, of its nature, reluctant to be tied down! "Anima" is a Latin word for spirit – it is the origin of such words in the English language as "animated" – giving life to. The parallel Greek work is "psyche", commonly translated as "soul", or "spirit", or "mind". Animism was an early human expression of thanksgiving for the animals, plants and trees, which gave up their life force to sustain human existence. Interestingly, both these nouns are feminine in their original language – so, probably unwittingly, some of the old men of the early Christian church introduced to their doctrine of the Trinity a third, *feminine* person!

From time to time, it was in the very ordinary, sometimes challenging, and yet simple settings that I have been enabled to take part in the truly wonderful. It has been in climbing mountains and reaching the peaks that I have felt the greatest humility and thankfulness, in riding on the mudguard of a Ferguson tractor cutting hay and laughing out loud.

I have enjoyed the almost familial friendship of many amazing people who were "religious". I could never have endured the many crises of my life had I not known they were there. Some have been charismatic and inspirational. Most are, like me, hopeful travellers. We committed our work to growing ourselves and nurturing that growth in those among whom we were appointed to serve. We were committed to living authentically and responsively outside the confines of Canon Law – perhaps beyond definition or explanation – having a genuine connection to the world around us.

Reading, storytelling, conversation – all play a part in the connecting of spirit. It is to be aware of an invisible thread connecting with and interlacing all the elements. I am sure there is a science somewhere for this. Maybe it is quantum physics? Spirit-filled sunrise – spirit-sensitive darkness. Is there anything without breath? *Water* has the essence of *air*; fish breathe in it. Pottered *clay* is *fired* into beauty. Connections across the face of the Earth – since the first *Breath* (Ruach) – belonging together. The four elements from Greek origins are earth, water, wind and fire.

That *ruach* is the Hebrew word for the "breath of God" which, in the book Genesis, animated the planet. It is the poetic way to picture the origins of our universe before we learned scientifically about the Big Bang and evolution. That same *ruach* is the breath of life in each human spirit. It may be also the "rushing mighty wind" experienced by church leaders at the first Pentecost. It is a very guttural word that approximates to how we Irish say the word "sheugh" (a ditch).

Our sense of belonging emerging from this universal breath is both sensual and compelling – total. Desire may offer something spiritual – anger certainly will. And maybe envy, too. Maybe all the Seven Deadly Sins have a spiritual quality? We have been conditioned to imagine that spirit is "goodie-goodie" stuff, born of light. The rest, darkness and badness, belong elsewhere. Perhaps we might think again about that.

Now I begin to understand that spirit is connected to *everything*. Is spirit "civilising" or is it crude – or both? Is it in the tree, and also in the blade that cuts it down? Spirit is in the flame that burns the wood. It is in the comfort and light the fire gives to those surrounding it. Our spirituality may be one thing *and* the other – and both at the same time. We cannot put a boundary around it in time or space.

Can you have spirituality without spontaneity? No, you *must* have spontaneity! And the moment you say that, it is gone. Once you make spontaneity a requirement, you have lost what you are looking for. That is the nature of this focus. The more you concentrate on it, the less attainable it becomes. Having a spontaneous moment often catches it unawares – and so it catches you unawares as well! We become open to just "letting it happen". As divine children – all of us – playing in a garden of goodness, we are attracted to each other because of what we see in one another. We are not mindful of what our parents and teachers believe or fear – we delight completely in what it is we share *now*.

Being the parent of 5 children was a reminder to me of the openness and naivety, which are characteristic of being young. Working with children at home, in a school setting or through the church, allowed me to experience and sense how easy it is for adults to lose our innate longing for fun and how readily we retreat into patterns of stress and distress. Relating to children seems to me to be an essential ingredient of this spirit-growing process. Whether you have your own children, or not, spend a little time with one or two children soon, with the sole purpose of being reminded of their unfailing optimism.

Which features would you *choose* to nurture and express your spirit? It *is* a choice. Maybe baptism, confirmation or bar mitzvah were impositions – now you are an adult you are free to choose.

Who is the most important person in your life? You might feel like answering: "God" or "Christ". If so, I will refer you back to the teaching that the divine is part of who *you* are. Even God is telling you that you are the most important person in your life!

I am reluctant to die. I long to live. My hope and expectation daily sideline any fear of dying – unless, of course, something shocking happens to stimulate the dying feeling. Certain events like the diagnosis of a serious illness, or a 9/11 crisis, Covid-19 or climate disaster will certainly raise the spectre of death. Still, I live. I am alive. I have not chosen to breathe – to be alive – but I do have a say in whether I go on or give up. Either says something about my spirit. I am hopeful; I can endure; I am in a terrible place right now; I have no positives left. Both these states are related – they are points along the one scale. As humans, we are prone to emotional and spiritual fluctuation. This is neither good nor bad – it just *is*. Darkness and light are at opposite ends of the same continuum – they belong together.

Now I will highlight some key components of the spiritual. How will they compare and contrast with those of religion? You are free to allocate these contrasting elements under the heading of *Spiritual* or *Religious* or both. You are also free to add or omit any items which you might choose to fit into your emerging pattern:

child-like	adult
fun	serious
openness	protectiveness
pain	suffering
subjective	objective
meaning	purpose
possibilities	certainties
I am	you are – thou art
reality	myth
inclusive	exclusive
vulnerability	strength
fusion	fission
individual	community
present	future and past
hope	fear
spontaneous	predictable
homoeopathy	allopathy
fluid	solid
pride	humility
darkness	light

By now you will be thinking of elements from your own experience – your own story. Give yourself permission to create, play and explore.

We may even set these contrasting factors down in such a way as to see a link between them, as though they are at differing stages of a sequence. This reduces the notion that the elements are in conflict, and that they may even complement each other in certain circumstances.

These are not all mutually exclusive factors; some are more prevalent on one side. Both can be important to each. It is just that, by separating the elements in this way, we can begin to understand how easy it is for our religion to sublimate our spirituality. Without performing this exercise, we can so easily assume that religion *does* provide for all our spiritual needs. Because religion can *not* do this, I have felt it necessary to put these ideas together. Once we have some insight into our spirituality, we can approach our religious communities with constructive proposals, based on our identified needs.

Different people are at different stages of growth. Some can imagine beyond the system, others are constrained by inherited patterns. There are no bad people in this, no wrong answers to worry about – only what is. We are good people together. We recognise each other's fears and limitations and trust that in the shared variety of our experience, we will all grow to new heights and increased confidence in the spiritual power that gives meaning to our lives.

At times in my life, I have noticed that I do not feel as though I am achieving very much. Not that I worry unduly about that! When I look back over such a time, I sometimes notice that the fallow period has allowed me to re-jig some of my thinking, to rearrange my priorities. Although this activity was mostly unconscious, it was a process of reordering the space in my life. I now call this behaviour "space engineering"! It is closely associated with listening in a connection with another person. I am offering space to allow her to do some useful engineering.

This might sound somewhat trivial to you, but I want to underline that there is an identifiable pattern to the growth of spiritual awareness. There are tools to assist with the digging down and the climbing up. It may appear random, yet there are connections between all the pieces. The reassuring thing is that at the very moment we feel a situation is impossible, the possibilities for resolution become visible, even if they are nowhere near what we had expected or hoped for. Surprise!

Putting a name on the "divine" has usually created conflict and division. Perhaps that is why the God of the Hebrews originally had an unpronounceable name – JHWH. Whatever terminology you are most comfortable with yourself is good enough for you to speak out loud in the company of others. The name you use is worthy of the respect of everyone else.

The "Kingdom of God" is a key term for Christians. I have had difficulty with this idea – it assumes a certain model for divine work with a hierarchical royal framework where God is at the top and we are near the bottom. I have wrestled with these words. "Kingdom of heaven" is no less problematic. So, I guess I will make do with the word "realm", using it as "in the realm of possibility". I will use the word "divine" instead of God – at least for the purposes of this spirituality construct. When we do this, we do not have to explain to people of any faith what we mean – it is about as inclusive as I can possibly make it.

For us, the "realm of the divine" influences our lives from within, spiritually, and externally from our religious or faith community. We can read whatever books we choose to nourish our wisdom. We can associate with individuals or groups to meet our need for camaraderie, encouragement and support. We may worship in a church, a mosque, a temple, a synagogue, a meeting house or a gurdwara.

We may rejoice in hymns ancient and modern, choral excellence, chanting or silence, in a religious format of our choosing. If we truly feel that walking in the woods or attending a rock festival is the best way to commune with the divine, there is only one person whose permission you need – *yours*!

As I stated earlier, growing up in Northern Ireland gave me a sense of religious division – how one side is "good" and the other "bad". You really had little choice about sitting in the middle or doing your own thing. I suspect that in Islam there are similar splitting characteristics between Sunni and Shiite, as between Catholic and Protestant. I am certain that in all cultures there are constraints that prevent us from expressing our personal spirit as divine.

The idea that membership of a religious group is adequate to meet our responsibility for where we are in life diminishes our subjective existence. Life is a series of actions – or inactions – all of which have consequences for us and others. When we do not express our personal requirements and challenge what we find unnerving, we sell short not only our own reality but the growth opportunity for the whole church or community. The first tenet of *all* religions should be to give thanks for challenge, curiosity and adversity.

When was the last time that you used the word "fun" to describe your religion? This helps us to sense the lightness of our spirit and expect to be uplifted. Fun means that we can be surprised, we can laugh and cry and play. Much of what is in religious life is too serious to allow for that. Humour seems to be an alien feature of many religions.

Many of Jesus' teachings contain challenging levity. I notice that he never referred to the "poor" as a lesser people – "The poor you will have with you always". He wanted to enable people to see that there is no meaningful starting point

– or ending – on this journey, without poverty. Yet our religious history shows a strong exclusive identity with the rich and powerful, and a disparaging attitude towards the poor.

We also look at how our spiritual instincts affect our relationships. Inevitably, we interact with other people – family, friends and strangers. Are we conditioned to accept over 51 per cent responsibility for any relationship or friendship we are part of? (Yes, of course, with children.) Can you see how easy it becomes for one person to take increasing responsibility for an entire relationship? If that is leading to exhaustion and dysfunction, there is a need to address the imbalance. This is just as vital for those Christians who talk about having a personal relationship with God or Jesus. Is God 100 per cent responsible for his/her relationship with them?

How do we relate to the people and organisations where we work, live and pray? Is there a feeling of being at the margin of the community – not quite fully accepted? There is no work, life or religious community where everyone thinks identically. There will be shared beliefs, and there will be very significant divergences. Are we willing to live with a variety that contrasts starkly with our own comfortable ideas? There is no requirement for uniform thinking. There may be common duties and responsibilities, and the sharing of these may need to be reviewed regularly.

During the second half of the twentieth century, we inherited some amazing poetry and music on the planet – writers like Pete Seeger, Bob Dylan, John Lennon, Paul McCartney and Leonard Cohen, among many others – who donated words and chords to our inheritance of wisdom. That the religious communities failed to incorporate much of that contemporary expression – and continue to do so – is a sign of their inability to adapt to the present.

We do not appear to have the capacity to reach out, to accept the gifts which are available to us in each generation. This is a substantial loss to religious communities – another door to exclude some of the healing that contemporary music, poetry and art bring to assist with our response to life's challenges.

Do we share a common reality with people we encounter casually? We won't know if we don't speak to them. If the colour of their skin, or the volume of their music, makes me hesitant about chatting with them, then I need to ask myself why. If they do not speak the same language or sing the same songs as I, do I need to explore how to build a bridge for us to communicate? Based on what I know of our spiritual needs, I'd say "Definitely – *yes!*"

Can we envision the time in our life when we will have nothing material, no belongings? Will that be poverty or riches? Will that come as a welcome shock to our system? It is important in our spiritual development that we learn not to fear death. We try to detach from our dependency on material things from time to time – by withdrawing to a place of quiet, or by giving away possessions that no longer meet our life requirements.

How prepared are we to hold to our personal spirituality when oppressed by our religious community? Will we just go along with the crowd, rather than take some flak for saying clearly what we feel? Faith will split and it will unify (fission and fusion) – can our spirit hold firm in the tension between these?

Because of my health challenges, I have explored and availed of the more subjective discipline of homoeopathy. This works because most diseases come from within our bodies, our minds, our emotions. When we receive the appropriate remedy, our bodies will be prompted to recover balance. Life Force, like our spirit, is individual and fluctuates according to the stresses on, and nurturing of, each part of our lives.

A homoeopathic practitioner does not have a simple fix for any given condition; each person must be assessed individually, taking a whole range of aspects into consideration. When we contrast this with the allopathy of conventional medical treatments, we can see how institutional 'care' can sometimes conflict with individual needs – not only in medicine but also in religion.

One size does not suit *every*one!

When Covid came, we began wondering how God could let this happen. I look back to the 1980s when some Christians said that AIDS was God's punishment on gay people – NO! NO! NO! Such a notion troubles my spirit deeply. I want nothing to do with a God who would use her spiritual power to cut off as worthless large swathes of humanity.

Let us focus on a spirituality that says we will each be safe in the world (from Covid) only when *all* are safe. Does that not sound like a wholesome, divine ambition? When I receive my vaccination, I do so not just for myself, but I do so for all humankind. When one of us is broken, we are all diminished. Until our spirit voices proclaim in unison the integrity of all humanity, across boundaries of belief and nation, then our faith communities have little more to offer than our own pathetic separate survival. Any religion which stifles the fun and spontaneity of living destroys much of what it purports to celebrate.

"Rarely do members of the same family
grow up under the same roof."
– RICHARD BACH

CHAPTER 3

I AM – Source of authority

I am one
I am indivisible.
As the sun, moon and stars
belong in the one universe
inclusive of the earth
and all else that is,
so my parts all belong
together in the universe.
I am.

I am the mother – I am the son
I am the father – I am the daughter
I am within – I am around
I am the tide – I am the welcoming shore
I am the rock – I am the encircling sea
I am the bird in flight – I am the sky
I am the cloud – I am the clearness
I am the soldier – I am the war
I am my despair – I am my hope
I am the beginning – I am the journey
and
I am the end.

With gratitude, I remember meeting so many people who convinced me of the wonder of living. They projected divine characteristics and wisdom, not necessarily in the words they spoke, or in their holiness, but in the ways they lived their lives and influenced mine so far – Jim Kemmy, Davy Burns, Ann Lynch, Khalil Kazi, Joe Long, Frank Gleeson – expressing thanks for what we have, rather than wasted longing for what we do not have.

The past is very present – the present is a gift and appears to be gone as soon as the next present moment arrives. This is the transient, ephemeral nature of spirit encounters. Our challenge is to experience our reality as it is happening. This means we need to develop the capacity to put the past in its place and to allow the future to unfold.

The alternative is that we spend lots of our time in the now, trying to ensure certain future outcomes. Of course, there is a trade-off in that we make plans for next week and later in the year, but the ability to be very present eludes us most of the time. Mindfulness is the key to this process. It is a universal spiritual discipline.

My story is history. *I am* the subject in my life – not a bit-player in someone else's. This is true for you too. Most of our early reading brings us princes and princesses who are always beautiful, brave and kind. They "rule kingdoms" wisely and show great generosity to "their people". Most of our school history is full of generals who won or lost, kings and queens who ruled with terror or kindness. The story is usually told from a top-down standpoint. The message is obvious – the important people in the world occupy the highest positions. Our history is so white, so male. It is about "winners". If you want to be important, then that is where we are taught to aim. I find that so depressingly distorted. That approach necessitates a lot of failures.

Again, if you speak about human rights or civilisation, there is an assumption that we in the West are leaders and the rest should want to follow where we go. Not the case! The presumption of being just and right, and having a monopoly on leadership, actually undermines the authority of the West to extend significant influence to others. How have non-western peoples survived so far without us? How rich is Africa? How much has western occupation despoiled its expansive resources?

Look at the culturally destructive forces of colonialism across the globe, as western empires for the past five centuries imposed alien values on civilised native peoples and cultures. For us to judge the performance of eastern nations through the lens of western values and our separate heavily biassed histories, is to assume that somehow we have got everything right, and they are in the wrong.

If we look at China, for example, and imagine a political system managing the logistics of caring for a population of 1.4 billion people, we will find things to criticise. Is there nothing to admire? I am in awe of a system that organises itself to meet the needs of all those people. Look at how they lifted millions of their people out of poverty over the past twenty years. In the West, there is much to cherish, and much to criticise. We would like to influence how China might develop different approaches to dealing with their ethnic minorities, or with climate change.

Perhaps instead, we could have a conversation with them in which we listen to *their* story. From there, we can appreciate each other's strengths and be open about our weaknesses. The current political ping pong judgement does little to encourage dialogue or dissolve misunderstanding. We look at societies and behaviours abroad, which are *different* to ours, but not necessarily *worse*. We often speak "You are..." as though we have yet to discover "I am...."

Of course, there are benefits from western influence in many areas of the world – India's civil service, the development of sports. There were pluses from the Roman colonisation of Europe and North Africa – what the Romans did for us! One effect of the Moorish invasions was to introduce Islam to the Iberian peoples in Southern Europe, *and* they brought a new level of culture through the establishment of many universities and libraries. Even the terrible invasions by Genghis Khan, as the Mongol Kingdom spread across Russia, China and most of Eurasia, east of the Caspian, brought additional benefits to trade and agriculture.

Generally, I am saying that colonisation damages the cultural fabric and essence of conquered peoples. The Irish, formerly a colonised people, have "colonised" many places around the world with Guinness and Irish stew, with good humour and a willingness to work hard. Their experience has been one of appreciation for being accepted into a new culture, and they have brought some of their own music, song and dance along. This is on a take-it-or-leave-it basis. I remember The Chieftains bringing out an album following their tour of China. They had discovered a commonality between the rhythms and tones of Chinese and Irish traditional folk music.

There is something invidious, however, about the economic invasion of cultures. This is exemplified by both China and the USA by their ceaseless pursuit of new markets. Just look at how western fast-food franchises in Asia have made many eastern people overweight and damaged their natural health. Now they are recipients of western-style allopathic medicine, which may give them a life extension of perhaps, 3 years on average, while they consume more and more drugs to counter the adverse effects of the ones they were given to remedy relatively minor complaints.

Western medicine is not the solution to all the world's health needs – check out Ivan D Illich's *Limits to Medicine*. Yet, allopathic research in China, the UK and the USA has enabled a prompt response in the form of vaccine creation to address the universal challenges of Covid–19. Polio has now been almost completely eradicated around the world. We are thankful for such capacity in the pharmaceutical world that has saved millions of lives.

There are long valid histories of healing in most societies, pre-dating modern medical practices. Quite a few old wives' tales included many successful treatments frequently derided by pharmaceutical corporations in their own interests. I remember my sister Sheelagh having ringworm on one of her wrists. Our mother brought her to a faith healer who administered a circle of ink (to all appearances) and mumbled some words. Within a few days, the condition had disappeared. My Grampa Stewart was the proprietor of Letterkenny's Medical Hall and people came regularly from all over County Donegal for one of his bottles. He never heard a complaint from any of them.

Often, the research in medical and social fields carried out here in the West cannot be trusted as holistic and balanced. The designer assumptions, which underpin the entire process of academic enquiry, are usually based on a paradigm that presupposes that the western model is best for the rest of the world too. That may well be true also of Chinese research – that its assumptions are made simply to confirm the expected outcomes. There was a joke told about the old USSR... a senior official announced to the Politburo, "Comrades, we'll have to postpone the election, I have mislaid the results!"

No, history begins with you – your story. *When* you were born and *where*. Did you have siblings? Later, you might even encourage your parents to recall the place and time when you were conceived! How you interacted within your family is important. Your story is a dynamic of truth and imagination. Your moments of light and darkness, wisdom and confusion, are just as crucial to our collective understanding of divine life as the stories of apostles and disciples in the Bible, or the pages of academic annals of history.

Sure, there *is* some history in The Old and New Testaments. It is often difficult for a casual reader to define where historical fact, myth and interpretation overlap. It is better not to assume that every word in the Bible is unerringly expressed by a very powerful divine who is infinitely greater than we are – even though we are told we are "created" to be just like him! Any history with meaning and worth must start from where *we* are.

Be wary when you hear leaders say: "History teaches us...". Their interpretation of a set of recorded events *may* lead us to a certain understanding. This will usually be in accord with the underlying assumptions they have about what is right/wrong or good/bad. Remember that history is written by the victors and you are receiving their "take" on the subject; not that history can ever be completely objective. Just keep an open mind on all such things. Check what facts are available and choose what makes most sense to you.

Our best understanding of the history of World War I came from the stories of individual soldiers who endured the struggle in trenches – and songs and poems from writers in that period, among them Wilfred Owen and Siegfried Sassoon. They shed a revealing light on the war room decisions of incompetent generals and the bickering of European royal families. How interesting to note that the Battenbergs became the Mountbattens in 1917, around the same time as the Saxe-Coburg-Gotha's became the house of Windsor!

You are the author of your story. You are the leader of your life. Not because I write it here, but because it is the underlying truth of "I am". And your story then interlinks with the lives of others and you build up a network of experiences of truth and awareness. This does not make us better than our forebears; it ensures that we do not allow ourselves to be perceived as inferior.

We discover at some point – as I did, for the first time, from Civil Rights activists I met in Minneapolis in 1967 – that originally we all came from Africa. Who kept that piece of historical information from us? You will not find that in the Bible. It was not on the A-level history curriculum either.

In this chapter, I want us to get a handle on the proclamation "I AM". It goes back to the Old Testament story of the burning bush in Exodus chapter 3. Moses asked the voice coming from the burning bush: "Whom shall I say sent me?"

"Tell them I AM sent you!"

I am fire (my interpretation); I am the burning bush; I am the voice that says, "I am".

Holy being is the source of spirit. Its seed is within all of life, including yours. When New Testament writers attribute to Jesus the words "I AM", there is a clear link with that holy voice Moses claimed to hear, a*nd,* I would suggest, it links to us in the present. "I am the way; I am the truth; I am the life". I am now completely the one I was created to be. We looked at the ego in an earlier chapter and acknowledged that to hold to a person-centred spirituality is no ego-trip. It is the opening of myself to ridicule, to delight, to pain and disaster, to being awash with the incoming tide as well as to be empty at its lowest ebb.

I AM is a state of acknowledgement and acceptance of divine presence in my life, in the life of each person, and in all living creatures around me. This is the realm of all that is holy – within the reality of all that is earthly. It takes a while for this to grow in me – but I am convinced that we are all I AM, individually and collectively. This is not the creation of a whole lot of messiahs – God forbid! – this is accepting the reality that our community *is* divine, with all the opportunities and delight that earthly living offers us.

By treasuring you, I AM. Being treasured by you, you are I AM. It is a dynamic that we unconsciously practise. When we give it voice, it allows us to recognise the power we can have in our lives – and how unhelpful it is for us to have power in the lives of others.

You did not have to go to university to gain this wisdom – it was always there in a structure that has deliberately occluded that truth so that you would be dependent on the services of the "professionals". It has been a conspiracy within the religious institutions to deceive and deprive the people, so the inadequate may be preserved and the mediocre celebrated. The hand-wringing over the great sacrifice of Jesus "giving his life for the world" cloaks the fear of risking all our inheritance on the present, the presents, the presence.

Of course, religion prompts the notion that you do not have to make this sacrifice yourself. I believe that the "once-for-all" teaching about Christ's sacrifice is misleading. It is referred to as the "scandal of particularity", that somehow one person, at one time, met the spiritual needs of all people for all ages, before and after his own lifetime. If we hold to that, then are we not depriving ourselves, in the present, of the authority to direct the course of our own lives?

Many will say "everything – externally – is in the hands of God". You may wish to continue believing that, but in such belief you must accept that probably half of the world's population in any age is getting a raw deal from this God. It is little comfort to them that they have not accepted Jesus into their lives – whether or not they have even heard of him. The truth is, you *do* have to make something of this your*self* in your own life – the vicar will not do this "vicariously" on your behalf.

Remember, if you have to deal with the moment of your death, then start taking responsibility for the moments of your living. Maybe this is a step too far for you just now, but let the seed grow for a while and maybe...?

No going Nowhere –
movement is necessarily within.
"I am" responsible
for the growing down,
to Earth, and out,
to Universe,
knowing there's no containing –
only letting go of– desire.

Underlying confidence in
what is.
I am.

When we explore what possibilities lie ahead for us in life, we are usually offered a religious roadmap, which requires a set of basic knowledge, possibly beginning with a catechism (preset questions/preset answers). That's really not exploring at all. In Christianity, there is almost a need to become a Jew in order to understand the faith. Of course, Jesus *was* a Jew, and so were all his early followers. Burdened with the weight of the Book means that there is little scope for spontaneity.

Where the Book – the Bible – says I AM, we are conditioned to understand that this is about God, not about me. My spirituality leads me to recognise I AM as the point of identity between divine being and myself. When, or if, Jesus used this term to describe himself – "the way", "the truth", "the life" – we are being shown how we might grow into this reality. So much of the language clearly expresses our oneness with the divine. This is a present reality, whereas the religious emphasis is, unhelpfully, on some future unification/ belonging. This reality is "present" both in the sense of *gift* and as *present tense*.

When Gandhi was asked what he thought of western civilisation, he replied:

"I think it would be a very good idea."

CHAPTER 4

Lessons from Prison

"You cannot separate the just from the
unjust and the good from the wicked;
for they stand together before the face of
the sun even as the black thread and the
white thread are woven together.
And when the black thread breaks, the
weaver shall look into the whole cloth,
and he shall examine the loom also."

The Prophet – KAHLIL GIBRAN

When I began working in prison, my initial spiritual response was, "Here, but for the grace of God, go I." I was regularly horrified by some things the young offenders told me – about what they had done to others *and* by what had been done to them. There was an obvious case for listening to *their* stories. Often in the role of Chaplain, there is an expectation to share the only story that is "important" – the Christian message. However, I soon learned that listening to the personal experiences of these young men generated a sense of relationship which was much more meaningful than that of a

Christian teacher. The *message* was in the listening. And the stories were authentic.

In a sense, prison casts offenders into inner darkness, underscoring their unworthiness. They are told that they deserve their punishment, and they should not forget that. Some people in such circumstances can forgive themselves and begin the delicate process of rebuilding their self-respect. My name... My number... What are my family and friends saying? How can I say I'm sorry? Am I sorry?

The institutions to which we commit offenders are managed hierarchically. They offer little in the way of corrective or rehabilitative treatment – not by design, more because of overcrowding. They can undermine the quality and integrity of the lives of many of the staff working in them. Over time, encountering people who have committed outrageous acts, the sense of shock is eroded and a "new normal" enters our consciousness.

The authority is at the top of the hierarchy, but accountability for the delivery of the "service" is at the landing officer level. Prisoners use this model to set up their own hierarchy: daddies and their captains at the top, weaklings and sex offenders at the lower end of the pecking order.

I was fortunate to work with several governors and prison officers who were committed to a process of consultation whereby prisoners could make known their concerns and issues. This meant that sometimes these interactions amounted to a prisoner "shopping list" – more benefits in one direction than the other. There was, however, a realisation among the inmates that progress was often limited by other institutional priorities, and that everything could not be accomplished immediately. The prison menu improved dramatically, with an element of choice, and consequently much less waste.

This coincided with improvements in management/staff relationships, where historically there had been much tension. This process was aided by the recruitment of many ex-miners following the 1982 Miners' Strike. These (men, mostly) brought a different skill-set compared to those who were selected previously, often following a career in the Army. These people had good organisational training and were responsive to the needs of a disciplined workforce.

The ex-miners had well-developed problem-solving skills, which helped them to identify *potential* trouble and intervene before issues became confrontational. Many had some emotional intelligence and came from communities where they instinctively looked after each other. I never asked an ex-miner what the difference was between going down the shaft to the coal-face and walking through the prison gate going to work.

A prison service has the responsibility to maintain a safe environment for the entire community. It has a duty to provide prisoners and staff with opportunities for growth and development. This demands that the prison service needs to ask questions regularly about its own values and priorities. In the 1990s, we had an interesting time working on our national and local mission statements – they helped us to focus our minds. However, that needs to be a process, not a once-for-all event. What an amazing group of people prison staff are – serving the people of the country, working among some of the most challenging offenders.

I hear Sean shout at me across the yard – "Hey, Pete, say a prayer for me. I'm up for parole next week."

"Say your own prayers, Sean", I tell him, without concern, continuing on my way.

"Oh, OK, Pete".

The visiting Assistant Chaplain-General waited until we arrived back in my office before he said to me: "Do you think you handled that interaction with compassion?"

"Well, Geoff, it's like this. Sean will not get parole. He is regularly in trouble with the staff, and he has refused to attend any offending behaviour course. If I pray for him, and he fails to get parole, he will blame me, or God, or anyone, before he takes responsibility for it himself. He will be shown a measure of compassion when he receives his parole knockback."

"Oh."

There may be little or no forgiveness from anyone – not from society, or even grudgingly from the church/faith community. But what about the love of God? Does it wipe clean the slate that records all the worst of my doings? Did I do nothing right? Is there anywhere a record of my goodness?

I often recall the story of the prison chaplain in the story of Malcolm X in America. Malcolm attended classes and studied the Christian faith until gradually he began asking questions.

"Was Jesus white?"

"Of course," came the reply.

"And did he have blond hair?"

"Yes, Malcolm – Jesus was a white man with blond hair."

On hearing those answers, Malcolm withdrew from his Bible studies and felt affirmed in his call to the Islamic faith.

People in prison have a highly developed "bullshit detection" capacity! There is little point in pretending that I have made a phone call or written a letter on behalf of an inmate. His "inside" intuition will inform him of the reality, and he will (will not) trust the chaplain again. So, when asked questions about faith or the Bible, an honest "I don't know" was often best. If your faith has some spiritual currency, it will emerge in the relationships you have – not in the words you speak.

The numbers of minority ethnic offenders sent to prison increased disproportionately from the early 1980s (up to 14 per cent of the prison population – almost twice that within the general population). The idea of a white orthodoxy would not have made sense, rather it would have been an obstacle. Prison communities comprise staff and inmates of varying races and creeds. A chaplain's role is to be there for the entire community – and to nurture a spirituality that is inclusive and joyful, real and challenging, in all quarters.

Now the Chaplain is not the only person responsible for this aspect of institutional life, but his job description rather sets him up as a leader. Some chaplains uncovered great spiritual awareness and faith in staff colleagues and among the inmates. It might seem strange to people in faith communities outside the prison walls to imagine that spiritual leadership might be exercised by a uniformed officer or a prisoner. Well, you have to try to make the best of the situation you are in. I am sure Jesus sometimes expressed disappointment with the bunch of men who made up the twelve disciples, but at least he got to pick his own crew!

Another culture change that came in the early 1990s was that female officers were posted to work in male prisons. This had a significant impact on lowering the levels of hostility and raised the whole challenge of how to be assertive, rather than dominant. Around the same time, women were employed as chaplains – but women had already been working for many years in male prisons as probation officers, psychologists, education staff and workshop instructors.

One Sunday morning I invited a group of young men to "confess our sins"... "You must be jokin', Pete," said one guy, to much laughter. So I asked why that was, and he replied, "I'm confessing to nothing – not in here!" We had a ten-minute discussion on how confession was understood in this community, and we agreed, quite readily, to use the term "Come clean" instead. That term continued to be part of any liturgy in which I shared, long after leaving prison work. It was refreshing to have in our worship something of the "vernacular" which we claim to use as our church language.

On another Sunday, "Lifer Brian" – who normally read a lesson – arrived after others had been allocated the readings. He was really disappointed and so I invited him to read the Gospel. The service began, then as Brian's turn came, it soon became obvious that he was a tad uncomfortable reading about Jesus' attitude towards divorce. As he progressed, he was visibly growing redder and redder in the face. Instead of finishing with "The Gospel of the Lord", Brian announced pompously in my direction: "Father, you gave me that reading deliberately. Well, you know I divorced my first wife and killed my second, and I certainly think divorce is much the better option." A statement that earned him a round of applause!

Worship and community in prison were about, "How do I grow as a person?", rather than whether I might get to heaven. Inmates sought out support groups and classes to explore how they had got into their mess in the first place, and how they could change their circumstances for the next time out. Alcoholics Anonymous was a popular meeting place to facilitate awareness of a "higher power", and to share in an honest expression of *my* addiction. Other activities, as well as formal education and offending behaviour groups, were offered to enable the inmates to address their thinking patterns.

I remember one offending behaviour group, called *Straightforward*, which Kate Jenkins facilitated with me. During the last session, when participants were invited to set at least one achievable goal, Eddie announced: "I will not do burglaries anymore" (since he had discovered how much suffering was experienced by families). "I will just do *commercials!*" We commended him on one level, but also challenged him on another. Sometimes we had to settle for tiny incremental gains.

Father Joe was the RC Chaplain who also worked in a parish in the community. He was a really lively spiritual man who was deeply interested in people. He once asked his Bishop if he could receive a grant to study Creation-Centred Spirituality for a year in America. The answer was "no". Undaunted, Joe took a part-time job with the local Post Office. He did the village round very early each morning to earn enough money for his future studies. One parishioner was overheard saying, "That new postman is a dead ringer for Fr Joe!". When the Bishop eventually heard about this, he was enraged and told Fr Joe that he would not visit the parish to administer Confirmation to the children – as a "punishment".

Some weeks later, I was just clearing my desk at work, about 8.30 in the evening, when the phone rang – "Pete, I've got a favour to ask you. I'm in serious shit, and I'm frightened of the devil. Will you meet me tonight?" This was Paul, a recently discharged prisoner who lived in Sheffield. I could not really go off to Sheffield so late that evening, but I asked him to get the next train to Donny (Doncaster), and I'd meet him at *The Leopard*, a pub near the railway station. When I saw Paul, he really looked frightened and exhausted. He showed me a gold ring, insisting that it had been "passed on" to him. It had churchy markings on it and probably belonged to a Bishop. I assured Paul that even if it had been stolen from a Bishop – and I was pretty certain that it had been – the thief would hardly go to hell as a direct result. A bit of "due process" would have to be negotiated before such an outcome!

He *pleaded* with me to return it to its owner – even though he could not tell me who or where they might be. He was trying to confirm that he had not actually been the one who had stolen it. I accepted it from him and reassured him that this was not the end of the/his world. He seemed greatly relieved just to have offloaded the item. Now I was the receiver of stolen property! At home that night, I had a more thorough look at the ring and deduced from the crossed keys that it was probably the property of the RC bishop. Had it belonged to the Anglican bishop I would probably have heard through the grapevine that he had been burgled.

The next day I called Joe to ask if his bishop had been burgled. "Yes, indeed," he said, "and the only thing of value that was missing was the bishop's ring." I filled him in on my news, and we met for lunch that day. On seeing the ring, he could confirm right away that it was indeed *the* item! I gave it to him, knowing that it would be returned safely to its owner. A week later, Joe indicated that all was well. In gratitude, the bishop now agreed to come to the parish for the Confirmation of the young people. Joe said that, as he left the bishop's house, he could tell that the old man wasn't completely certain if Joe had orchestrated the whole affair or not!

You will now know this is a very permissive approach to developing a religious community. Our focus was primarily on *my* story rather than the God story, and a person-centred spirituality before a God-centred one. You would expect that this might lead to disaster and losing a traditional sense of the "church", but you would quickly dismiss your misgivings if you attended the worship – on Sunday mornings and Wednesday evenings – when the sense of participation, challenge and delight penetrated the culture and finds expression in singing and attentiveness, and a sense of belonging.

The important thing I discovered through all this is that the spiritual teachings of my Christian upbringing about Incarnation, Crucifixion, Resurrection and Ascension are not necessarily "events" but "processes". Here in the prison community I was observing the human and divine together (Incarnation); people at their crossroads of life (Crucifixion); the determination and optimism to struggle up off the floor and try once more (Resurrection); flying kites of hope and ambition to reach the mountaintops (Ascension). Here in the present is a crucible where the spiritual is evident in the reality of people's lives.

Redemption and *salvation* have been the cornerstone of evangelistic Christian teaching for decades. They are merely words to acknowledge a buy-back clause in our life process where we come to terms with the bad choices we have made to date. We realign our compass for the road ahead (redemption). Healing (salvation) is a process of recovering our well-being after suffering the unbearable distress of losing our way and hurting others *and* being hurt and broken ourselves.

Incarnation is a religious word for the integration of humanity and holiness. For Christians, this is seen in the person of Jesus of Nazareth (Messiah). I understand and accept that there is a historical Jesus of Nazareth, whose death was recorded by the Roman historian Tacitus. Some unflattering references were also made about him by the Jewish historian Josephus. All the Gospel narrative does is provide us with a loose biography that was written *from* people of faith *to* people of faith.

Jesus offers us an example or paradigm of how all humanity is a unity with the divine. If this union has any real merit, it is to challenge us to develop our humanity into higher and deeper realms. Climbing mountains and deep-sea diving are practical ways in which we can express these aspects of our nature. Our fresh thinking cannot be contained within "old wineskins". Incarnation is a *two-way* process – the divine entering the realm of humanity, and the human entering the realm of God. They do not teach you this at theological college! It requires flexibility and courage to grow in faith – to become everything that we are in embryo.

Crucifixion is an intrinsic part of our development. It is a series of crossroads and choices which form career choices and engage life-partners; it is the place where we are confronted with the challenge to grow or die. And dying is not the end either, because *resurrection* is a key component of this process too. Not that we play around with "flatlining", as in an ICU in the local hospital – it is a growing awareness that we are part of something dynamic and transforming, not just momentarily, but in an ongoing, "eternal" mode.

Easter is not so much an *event* as a process of continuing emergence: not dissimilar to creation (recreation). And that, interestingly enough, brings us round to the notion of re-birth, which is expressed in different religious communities in varying ways – from the doctrine of reincarnation to life cycle, to resurrection. There is very little new, or surprising, in any of these concepts, but when we put them together, we can begin to sense how all human spirituality is imbued with the idea of life being changed – transformed.

We, *each of us*, must greet our moments of death and resurrection repeatedly in differing circumstances as the process of our transformation!

Ascension brings us back to the mountains – and what a key part they play in our spiritual mindset. This has both passive and active dimensions, where we lift or are lifted according to our needs of the moment. It is a recurring theme within our spiritual development, a process that ensures we have the resources to encourage others to rise above the limitations of human existence. And, if we choose, we can feel that sense of divine glory within our own floundering lives.

In the New Testament, the Ascension image parallels the story of Transfiguration – an occasion when three disciples saw Jesus' face light up in the presence of Moses (The Law) and Elijah (The Prophets). This is an expression of faith that he was raised up to heaven, or that heaven came to meet us here on earth. Again, there are comparable stories in other faith traditions, which would suggest that this was a figurative rather than a historical event. There was, of course, the Elijah story in Judaism, and, from Hindu tradition, there is Arjuna, who was accompanied by Matali as they were carried up to heaven in a chariot.

Prisoners, unless they were on remand, were "guilty". Despite what you might imagine, very few men I encountered over those twenty-one years ever claimed they were innocent. Of course, some blamed their mothers, fathers, brothers, sisters or the Legal Aid solicitor, but they were not pretending to be innocent. There is a lot of guilt in prison – and outside as well. Many people carry around an oppressive amount of the stuff. It blocks their ability to delight in living. Well, I found a place where guilt can be appropriately discharged – a waste bin does the job admirably.

Can anyone tell me what value guilt feelings have for us? Do they do anything to improve the world or people's lives? Are they a necessary component on the path to acknowledging mistakes? I do not think so. It is really a way in which we oppress ourselves internally – beating ourselves up and making it impossible to grow beyond. Saying "Sorry" needs no framework, no explanation – just recognition of my mistake.

The idea of "wrong" being something each human is personally responsible for is a visible sign of our frailty and a reminder that we are growing. Not that we are somehow un-worthy, as though there is some great objective "worthiness" for which to strive. There *are* events along the way, but it is the evolving dimension, the movement, that we need to keep in focus. We should be thankful to Darwin for opening up for us the awareness of evolution as a model of how we develop – in all dimensions.

> "Two men looked out from prison bars
> One saw mud – the other saw stars."
> – *DALE CARNEGIE*

CHAPTER 5

—

Christianity, Church and Bible

"The supreme triumph of reason
is to cast doubt upon its own validity."
– Miguel de Unamuno

C hristianity has not served its followers well in the development of spirituality. Many leaders have claimed a special set of insights (Gnosticism) to keep them ahead in the divine pecking order. "Gifts are for giving" – as my friend Brian often said. Churches vest the control and teaching of spirituality in holy professionals. As a result, it may be accessed by the masses only by attending a range of rituals. This is a manipulation of the gifts rather than an offering or a letting go.

Assumptions – basic or complex – lie at the heart of every religion. Christian leaders have damaged spirit by their reluctance to question these assumptions. The claim that in Matthew 28:19, Jesus commissioned his followers to "go into all the world baptising in the name of the Father and the Son and the Holy Spirit" is not good news – it is *fake* news!

This biblical verse is a much later addition to the text. When the Gospel of Matthew was written (probably AD 85), baptism was in the name of Jesus only. The Trinity terminology came *much* later. This information does not surprise those who have studied the New Testament, but it has not been widely shared across the church communities. Why? Because leaders have colluded to maintain the notion that the Biblical writings are above question. "My people could not cope with that", I hear some of my erstwhile colleagues say.

So *please* do not regard this "great commission" as gospel and an authorisation to go over the Earth rubbishing the cherished spirituality of other peoples. Their inheritance has so much to offer to *our* wisdom. This verse from Matthew, like others, has been adapted/inserted to fit into the narrative of later years. The church controlled these writings to ensure that their leadership would be beyond criticism, evaluation or question.

I have been challenged over the years by conservatives who say: "This is not a democratic organisation, where the people vote for leaders or constitutional change!" I know – it is an authoritarian institution. It wields disapproving power in people's lives. It sets them up to be the object of negative judgement in the name of a loving God. Many church leaders feed their people half-truths and confused interpretations of past events.

They sideline or simply deny any science which might undermine their power and influence. Ask Copernicus or Galileo. They'll tell you! Charles Darwin held back publishing his theories on evolution out of respect for his devout wife's faith. Even in the nineteenth century, the church disapproved of any questioning of inherited dogma.

Conspiracy theories are not alien to the church – having just mentioned Copernicus for one! The Earth was the absolute centre of the universe *and* flat, and don't you go around pretending it is otherwise. The three-decker universe of Heaven above Earth, and Hell below, still structures the thinking of many followers today. And if it suits people to believe that, I will not rubbish their choice. To proclaim it as fact leaves me distinctly uncomfortable, and to teach that to children is a travesty. Furthermore, it says to the people of the world that we are opposed to critical thinking. For the record, I understand that we live in a *solar* system and all planets are more or less spherical.

Creation is an area where many conservative evangelical Christians have rejected the science. First of all, there is evidence of creation myths in many religions. The cosmic egg motif is a major symbol in creation myths, occurring in all parts of the world. Ancient Egyptians saw it as the soul of primaeval waters from which creation emerged.

One Chinese creation myth describes a huge early egg containing the first being, the giant Pangu. The egg broke and Pangu then separated chaos into the many complementing opposites of the yin and the yang, the essence of creation itself. There are two or three creation stories in Genesis. Much of this mythology was part of an oral (spoken) tradition long before it was written down. There is no suggestion in the texts themselves as to the date of the origin of the Earth or the Universe.

In the seventeenth century a Church of Ireland leader, Archbishop James Ussher, promoted a theory that the earth began in October 4004 BC. He was using a classical understanding of the sequence of the books of the Bible – and creating a template by which to timetable the events. He was wrong. He may have been working on the likely dates when the books of the bible were actually written. Today, many Christians regard his assertion as "truth" and use it to subvert Darwin's theory of evolution, which has at least valid scientific evidence to support it.

To propagate the idea that the Earth was created in 4004 BC is offensive to reality. It requires children to choose between science and religion. There is even an edition of the Bible (Schofield Version) in which the Ussher dates are inserted alongside the text. That is clearly an addition – certainly *not* "the Word of God". For me there is no debate – our spirituality is at least as wonderful with the Big Bang theory as it ever was with the wonderful Genesis mythology! Evolution is just as fascinating as the tales of the Old Testament. What are you so scared of? Bishop Ussher got it wrong. Get over it!

Children (and adults) under such influence have been expected to deny the evidence presented by science so that it will not contradict this particularly narrow interpretation of the origins of the planet. Carbon dating and other tools of archaeology help us get some measure of the time and times from which our written inheritance comes. It is unlikely that many of the Genesis stories, for example, were exclusive to the Jewish tradition.

In the Garden of Eden story there is the incident whereby the newly created occupants ate the forbidden fruit from the Tree of Knowledge. This led to the divine punishment of all human beings *forever* for human *disobedience* (according to Christian teaching). Jewish people used these texts for centuries before Christianity, but their understanding has been that the "sin" was to cloak their humanity, as though they could hide their genitalia from God. Very different interpretations! Hardly the basis for a doctrine of Original Sin?

St Augustine, a very human being, divined the doctrine of original sin from this Christian interpretation of humans relating to the creator. So, for fifteen centuries babies have been baptised to "wash their sin away". This belief presumes that all humans are intrinsically "sinful" from birth. How can you behold the wonder and beauty of the arrival of your child on Earth, and hold to a teaching that proclaims original sin?

In 1983, Rev Matthew Fox, a former Catholic priest, now Anglican, published a refreshing book, *Original Blessing*, challenging what St Augustine had taught. This book is a gift to the churches and was a very personal gift to me. What sort of creator would manipulate his work to produce such human inadequacy? Thank you, Matthew Fox, for your insight and blessing.

The Bible is a book. In fact, it is a library of books. It is meant to be read. It is not the divine plan for the people of God. Nor is the Old Testament a legal document that guarantees the ownership of the state of Israel for Zionists. It is a very select set of books, which excludes many others. Early church leaders were not happy with some of the content of other gospels and letters. A Muslim imam friend of mine, Khalil, once gave me a copy of *The Gospel according to Barnabas*. Thomas, Peter, Judas and Mary Magdalene have gospels attributed to them too. What were the criteria for inclusion/exclusion?

Again, regarding Matthew Fox, the men of the church did not want Jesus to be seen as a Sufi or spiritual teacher. That was well beneath where they had elevated him. Nor could any suggestion of Jesus having human vulnerability be promoted. That he might have been "interested" in Mary Magdalene was apparently unacceptable to them. This denial by holy men led in part to the repression of sexual desire in such a way that acts of procreation would only be "allowed" within matrimony.

Children of encounters outside of marriage have been systematically denigrated, as though they had asked for it – right up to the present day. If you have problems entertaining the teaching around the Virgin Birth, where does that leave

Jesus? At the very least, he was conceived outside of wedlock. Another dysfunctional family, thank God!

We vilified the innocent and let the conspirators and manipulators off the hook. Mother and baby homes in Ireland were a national disgrace. This has been well documented. The maltreatment of young mothers and their offspring was an accepted practice by all churches. But I am sure we found verses in the Bible to justify our shocking mistreatment of these women and their children. Note how the men got off the hook.

Leaders lost their sense of reason around the real-life issues of ordinary (human) church members. This created a fear of authority and the denigration of women. Even in my early years of ministry in the church, all mothers were still required to be "churched" after giving birth – "cleansed of impurity" – before being admitted to Holy Communion. What a disgraceful thing to do – bring a child into this world! You really couldn't make this up.

Such teaching and practice, I fear, infantilises community members and leaves them with a certain unreality around their faith. Christians have put so much emphasis on the Book, without applying reason and common sense to the content. If the God of the Old Testament behaved in the twenty-first century the way he is recorded as having behaved in the past, he would be charged with genocide and war crimes. We need to re-imagine our relationship with the "history" of the Old Testament, and much of the New Testament as well. By being open to new understandings, we might receive some helpful insights and deeper wisdom.

"Son of God" is not a term Jesus uses to describe himself. When Muslims – who venerate Jesus in much the same way as Christians – say Jesus did not claim to be Son of God, you have to agree with them. The New Testament texts do not record Jesus as making this assertion. His self-description of choice was "Son of Man". If we *choose* to believe in Jesus as the Son of God, that is a matter of *faith*, but it is not corroborated by the text of the Bible *as fact*. Jesus used the "Son of Man" term frequently so that his followers might rejoice in being human, not despair at how short we fall of the highest standards.

When some Christians use quotations from the Bible, they say it is the word of God. It is indeed many words about God – and even in some places alleged quotes of the great divine being: "Thou shalt have no other gods before me". (What was it I said about ego?) It is a lot of mixed material which belongs to the minds and the times of the people who wrote it.

How could we have sat idly by in the last century while white South African churches used verses in Acts 17 and Deuteronomy 32 to justify apartheid and the denigration of the native black Africans and people of colour? Yes, the devil can indeed quote scripture to her own advantage. Even Gandhi, as a young lawyer in Pretoria, was asked to leave a "whites only" church at a time when he was interested in the teachings of Jesus.

What I am saying here about the Bible and the church is not new. We were taught this basic information when I was a student over 50 years ago. I know that many of my contemporaries were not happy with the critical approach taken by (Professor) Freddie Vokes towards, particularly, the New Testament texts. His unlikely *cri de coeur* was: "We just don't know"!

So, the value of much academic learning never left the university setting. Given the extreme divisions over sexuality, creation, body rights and biblical interpretations, it seems important to me that we set down *reality* markers. We may, of course, choose to proceed blindly, with deaf ears, into oblivion. I suggest we need to come clean and be clear about what faith is, and how the institutions have been dishonest with us in the sharing of the messages.

I will throw in a teaser here, something that has distracted me for many moons. In Aramaic, the language spoken by Jesus, "Bar" means son: "Abba" means father. When Barabbas (son of the father) was released to the baying crucifixion crowd, was he the same person as Jesus (Son of the Father), or was he someone else entirely? I draw attention to this because I find more questions than answers in the source material of the faith. I do not understand it when a Christian refers to the bible as a "map for life", elevating the texts to some supra-academic realm beyond discussion or challenge.

Another example of a Christian conspiracy theory is from my home city of Limerick. In the first decade of the twentieth century, there was a Redemptorist priest, Fr Kray. He asserted that Jews and the Masonic Order were nurturing a nest of devils in a cave beneath the Rock of Gibraltar to destroy the Catholic church. He preached this message to full congregations for over a week.

Within several years, two Jewish synagogues in Limerick had been destroyed by fire, and all Jewish families had left the city. Religion has a responsibility to be honest with its people, even at the cost of the institution. There is absolutely no good reason to facilitate the perpetuation of lies and half-truths. To do so is to undermine the value of the faith professed.

And this same organisation teaches that the Church *is* the people! Can we begin to square this circle by trying to accept how *subjective* a spirituality needs to be to accommodate the wide-ranging needs of its membership? Managing change in lives is supposedly what the church is offering – but just suggest that the organisation itself needs to change/be changed, and you will face heels dug deep in resistance.

The issue I have here is that religions promote a spirituality that is "one size fits all". You take the historical package as a whole, and your spirit-growth is constantly frame-worked by that model. Almost as though an agreement was reached among some members of the hierarchy that "we'll get away with as much as we can, with as many people as we can... and we'll see how that works out". Well, accountability time has come!

The Anglican Communion has a variety of liturgy in different locations – cathedral choral settings, low-key rural parish worship with recorded music, family/children's services. However, the emphasis is common – the Creeds are common, the Prayer Book is common, the Holy Book is common, the totally anachronistic *39 Articles*[5] are common. The layout is fairly uniform – all facing forwards towards the priest.

The Roman Catholic Church has many common requirements around doctrine and practice. They have also developed a rich range of spiritualities through the religious orders and communities that have emerged over the centuries. The most notable of these are the Benedictine, Franciscan and Ignatian traditions. Celtic spirituality has blossomed through Clonmacnoise, Lindisfarne and Iona, as well as many other locations in Britain and Ireland.

Quakers, possibly because they tend to be smaller communities, worshipping in silence, often in a circle or horseshoe layout, afford space for individual reflection and awareness of the divine. This allows for greater variety and imagination. There is very little emphasis on insisting that we are all the same, *or* that we need to believe the same.

Regarding gender/sexuality – it seems clear from my little understanding of genetics that:

Parthenogenesis – "virgin birth" (not scientifically impossible) will produce female offspring only.

There is a blend of male and female genes and chromosomes in each person *on a sliding scale*: so it is hardly surprising that all men are not 100 per cent masculine, nor all women 100 per cent female.

Up to 50 per cent of men are more like their mothers than their fathers, and up to 50 per cent of sons (not necessarily the *same* men) would probably prefer *not* to be like their fathers. I make this observation as a son, and as a father. Perhaps it is similar for daughters and mothers.

While we are exploring gender issues, I would like to focus on situations where men are treated differently to women. For example, the term "domestic violence" usually refers to harm that men do to women. My experience and insight would suggest that much domestic violence is perpetrated by women on men, and by women on women and men on men in same-gender relationships. When I hear of and read about "gender-based violence" programmes, I can usually predict that these are about protecting women, regardless of the suffering experienced by men.

Similarly, with the term "genital mutilation", used in the press and in religious circles, there is the presumption that this is a female-only issue. While it is not so disabling, male genital mutilation goes on unchallenged in many cultures, often with religious approval (or even requirement), and such practice is unquestioned. Where are the campaigns to challenge this behaviour which can have significant ill effects on young men?

At this stage, I am not making a judgement about the merits or otherwise of these practices. I am raising the issue of why it appears acceptable to differentiate between actions that invade and diminish female and male lives. However, I do acknowledge here that the long-term damage to females is much more destructive.

The churches have treated women abominably. They have deliberately misused biblical texts to promote the idea that women are somehow inferior in the faith community and in society. They have blamed women for the "incident" in the Garden of Eden. Whatever human weakness is evident in females has been interpreted as confirming their unsuitability for high office in the church. In 2015, when the Church of England synod finally passed the vote that women might become bishops, one female Anglican was heard to proclaim: "At last women have broken through the stained glass ceiling!"

This legacy of discrimination against women for centuries has affected men too. It has left many men with a disproportionate sense of responsibility for decision making – a form of oppression, which has created dysfunction for men, and between the genders. While the changes of recent decades are to be welcomed and celebrated, there is still room for a lot of mutual appreciation and trust to grow between men and women in the churches and other faith communities.

Men must learn new skills and insights to develop emotionally and psychologically to meet the demands of this new reality. In response to male domestic violence, women's groups taught their members assertiveness skills. I believe that for men to change from dominant patterns of behaviour, we also need to learn assertiveness as an appropriate alternative means of expression.

The Roman Catholic Church has to meet significant challenges here – they cannot be postponed indefinitely, as the pressure mounts. They may ordain women since there is a shortage of vocations among men in many countries. Even if that were the reason, they would still have to find a theological framework in which to justify such a move.

The abolition of compulsory celibacy needs no such theological adaptation, just the rescinding of an edict or two and the reordering of finances to accommodate the needs of clergy families. Having gone to such lengths for so long to exclude women, and force celibacy on men, they really have backed themselves into a corner. The clock is ticking.

Women will also hopefully refrain from using the male "model" of leadership by which men clung on to control the organisation. We men have certainly screwed up the church; yet we are still permitted to share in the work of consulting, appraising needs, and renewing and restoring trust in relationships within our faith traditions.

Organised religions need to be mindful of the impact of such policies and practices on their dedicated and committed membership. They must be willing and prepared to adapt to the needs of their people in the present time. A new age demands a fresh vision.

> "New wine must be poured into new
> wineskins."
> – *ST MARK'S GOSPEL* 2:22

ENDNOTES

5.   The 39 *Articles of Religion* are the rules, regulations and practices that form the basis of the Church of England after the English Reformation. These Articles are found in the Book of Common Prayer that is used by most churches of the Anglican Communion around the world. As well as affirming some traditional universal Christian teaching, they include statements against some teaching and practices of the Roman Catholic church, and extreme protestant positions (viz. Anabaptists).

CHAPTER 6

—

Buddhism, Islam, Judaism, Paganism and Atheism

It was during my early days in prison chaplaincy that I first encountered Western Buddhism. Most of the people who came in to provide teaching and meditation classes in Buddhism were English and had learned about Buddhism in their adult life. They were not completely immersed in the cultural dimensions of that faith, but rather embraced its intellectual aspects. They enjoyed the contemplative experience, and many were excellent teachers of meditation.

Fluent Fuengsin[6] flowing
as a stream running clear
through confusion.
Sowing seeds of understanding
unifying words to challenge
division... and disinterest.

Vision: Practice: Meditation:
good reflective hesitation.

Later, monastic communities of Buddhists were set up in England, and spiritual leaders from the east either visited or became residents. I met several monks – from England and overseas – and was impressed by their commitment to work in prisons, and their human compassion.

Whether or not Buddhism is a "religion" is of little relevance to me here. It has a history 500 years older than Christianity and comes from the Hindu religion – older again! If you do not find a God in this faith tradition, then you will still uncover deeply devout practice and a holy, mindful focus, which I identify and appreciate as divine influence.

Buddhism trains its adherents to take responsibility for their actions – to accept the consequences, whatever they may be (Karma), and grow towards enlightenment (Nirvana). This religion, or philosophy if you prefer, is very individual, but also nurtured in community, most obviously in monasteries.

Lantau Monastery, on one of Hong Kong's islands, offers free vegetarian meals to passing strangers and visitors. It is one of many religious communities which express their spiritual growth in the feeding of thousands. "Annalakshmi on the Swan" is an Indian restaurant in Perth, Western Australia, where you may eat for free, or donate an amount you consider appropriate for the meal, according to your economic status – "Pay as you wish and as you can". For years, the Whitefriars in Aungier Street in Dublin have provided meals for homeless people in the city. "The Kitchen" in Carlow offers free lunches 5 days a week for those in need – the work of Graiguecullen Catholic church.

Faith communities, at their best, can offer relational (as distinct from transactional) encounters. Not necessarily for *life* – but for this moment. There is so much on offer, and we choose to accept what suits us best – at that moment. We are best friends – now! We may fall out forever – tomorrow. Our journeys may diverge significantly, and we may never meet again. These relationships, which are so vital and important *and* energy-filled, may be ephemeral and transient, ebbing and flowing like the tides.

I am currently privileged to live in a country where most of its citizens are Buddhist. When I went to do my driving test, I was required to watch a video in English, covering the essentials for safe driving. What struck me most was that the car's horn should only be used to make other drivers aware of your presence, *not* to give out to or censure the other. Unsaid was the truth that if you are angry with another person's driving, then treat that as your own problem, not theirs! I watch this attitude acted out on the roads and streets I use every day. Even in the sticky, sweltering, gridlocked streets of Bangkok, this restraint is evident... most of the time!

Another feature of this society is how "service" is offered. You can pay a lot of money for a restaurant meal – or very little. The same goes for hotel accommodation. A massage will usually be very affordable. Medical services, whether public or private – expensive or lower-priced – *all* these are offered with mindfulness, not dependent on the price tag. It seems that Buddhism teaches people to take pride in service – not being meekly submissive, but sincerely offering their skill, or role, as a gift to the recipient.

However, these anecdotal experiences cannot be applied to society generally without further research. Enough to say that I am impressed by the enabling influence of Buddhism over a society, to the benefit of the people and their interactions with others.

"Karma" is a key component of this, acknowledging that our behaviour has consequences – beneficial and harmful. This is a more adult concept than the Christian obsession with "right and wrong". It prompts an acceptance of reality, whether caused by my behaviour or others, and acknowledges that consequences are not always bad. Even in disaster there are excellent lessons to be learnt.

This does not imply that Christians need to develop a fresh approach to people of other faiths, just a more generous understanding of the unhelpful polarisation of *our* history of faith. Perhaps we inherited that from Greek dualism. Who knows? But we ought to be mindful of the impact such an inheritance has had on our thinking and our practice.

"Nirvana" is the pinnacle of this faith. It is both everything and nothing. It is riches and poverty. It is a heaven, not of place but of state. It is complete understanding and enlightenment, and it is complete emptiness. It is not unusual for young males in Buddhist countries to spend residential time in a monastery as part of their spiritual nurture. They assimilate the wisdom by experiencing the community life.

In the prison setting there was almost always at least one inmate who registered as Buddhist. It was our responsibility, and privilege, to provide a "chaplain" to come and visit regularly. Because of the undoubted benefit of meditation, other prisoners would ask to join the weekly "group". Some inmates registered as Buddhist on a purely pragmatic basis, and why not! For them the meditation became a high point in their week, initiating a lifelong practice. If the Buddhist chaplain could not attend, an inmate would lead the group.

The other dimension which attracted participation was the total acceptance, and lack of judgement. If I compare this to a group led by a couple of evangelical Christians, there would be a similarly social benefit, and mutual respect. However, the Buddhists would often grow to accept responsibility for how they came to jail – the Christians would more often blame the devil.

This is the point where *person-centred* spirituality finds its focus. In Christian communities, the total focus of spirituality is Christ-centred. So, when you get that out of focus, you become "bad" and need repentance. With Buddhism – and my proposed person-centred spirituality – you accept that the picture becomes blurred from time to time as you take your eye off the ball! That is just the way life is – and you make adjustments from within your own capacity to address how you have wandered. You refocus on the present.

If you wish to grow spiritually, then you take the leading role in your own life. When your story is told, you are the author. Of course, there is an element of the ego in all this. And we must take responsibility in acknowledging ego and managing it to achieve the best we can give to – and receive from – life. Ego does not disappear because we deny it or ignore it. It is part of our make-up. The more attention we give to incorporating it into the whole person we are, the greater our human integrity. The ego reminds us that we are subjects in our own lives – not objects in the lives of others.

Buddhism is not totally a *Peace* faith. I have heard of Buddhist monks who have resorted to violence regarding the protection of sacred buildings. I saw it reported that some monks have burned themselves alive as part of a protest. I know that a national army in a Buddhist state will bear arms and sometimes act violently. In Myanmar 2021, some monks appear to be supportive of the military dictatorship, others are opposed. It is the development of *inner* peace which is so important as a prerequisite to growing deeper and higher as a person. Buddhists practise their faith mindfully and peacefully.

The *Jewish faith* greeting "Shalom" is clearly a proclamation of Peace. Whether that Peace is exclusive to the people of the faith, or to be more widely extended, appears to depend on which sector of Judaism you encounter. In the prison context we sometimes enjoyed the company of Rabbis, or other leading members of the local synagogue, on the occasions of Festivals. Very few people registered as Jewish, but as we tried to build a common, multi-faith approach to prison chaplaincy, we naturally included Judaism as integral to that aspiration.

I have to say that for a people immersed in the Old Testament, most Jewish people I have encountered practise their faith with a levity that evades most Christians. Jews appear to have a comfortable relationship with the divine and enjoy jokes and very human conversation with him, and about him. The prison kitchens dreaded catering for Jewish feasts because any utensils used for non-kosher food could not be used to prepare or serve kosher meals. To ensure maximum compliance with the requirements, it was often preferable to "buy in" pre-packed meals from a suitable approved outlet to serve the needs of the relatively small number of prisoners involved.

When Jews read or listen to the story of the Garden of Eden, they do not conclude that it was human disobedience that led to the *exclusion* of Adam and Eve – rather, it was the application of fig leaves to the genitalia which suggested that they were now aware of their power to procreate. And that they were cloaking their humanity from divine eyes. This seems to afford a much healthier rapport with the creator God than Christian disobedience has done. So, were humans dismissed from the garden because they were naughty children, or because they had become aware of their power?

In recent years, it has seemed somehow "anti-Jewish" to disagree with the policies of the Israeli government. This is nonsense. Many Jewish people in Israel and around the world find the Zionist agenda of Netanyahu and others offensive.

Their voices must be heard too. Unfortunately, the politically correct sector of western democracies appears unable to distinguish between "anti-Semite" and "anti-Zionist". In the end, the tenets of Islam and Judaism are mutually provocative and are available to governments to manipulate as they will, in pursuit of their own power agendas. Person-centred spirituality eat your heart out!

Islam is a faith of Peace – As-salamu alaykum! This greeting means "Peace be upon you". It is the responsibility of each member of the community to read the Qur'an. Communal prayers in the mosque are encouraged – except on Friday when it is obligatory to attend the Jumma. Prayers are to be said five times each day. There is great clarity in Islam – right and wrong, good and evil. Interestingly, there is also a wide interpretation of the content of the Prophet's teachings.

"Jihad" is literally the "struggle". However, depending on which scholar speaks, Jihad can mean either the *internal* personal struggle or the struggle abroad between the faithful good and the evil infidel. Here, again, we find that fission, that dualism which religion can impose. In recent years, the latter interpretation has prevailed, at least in the eyes of many westerners, leading to an "us vs them" polarity, which in turn has led to suspicion and misunderstanding.

A permissive US policy towards Israel has an almost direct effect on the temperature of the tensions. The more Israel feels free to violate the Palestinian territory, the stronger the reaction from Muslim extremists. This is a clear indication of "cause and effect". Extremist violence often dominates these faith communities, despite their proclamations of Peace. When a tipping point is reached, the entire community is perceived by outsiders as hostile. Individuals are then treated as though all are extremists.

In Western Europe, much of Islam is intertwined with Middle Eastern and Pakistani culture. In prison, this was evidenced by the demand of many Muslim prisoners for spicy food – as though that in itself was a faith factor. However, we quickly had to come to terms with the need to provide halal food products. Imams were recruited to lead the Friday prayers and provide some faith context to young men who mostly had little or nothing to do with their religious communities outside of prison. Many of these inmates insisted, inappropriately, that their Qur'an should be treated with more respect than the Bible. Sayings from the Hadith (the Prophet's personal writings) were regarded by some as equally authoritative as the Qur'an itself.

Khalil Kazi, our imam at Leeds Prison, reassured us that if you consulted 4 or 5 different imams or teachers about the understanding of aspects of the faith, you'd be likely to get 4 or 5 different interpretations. When prisoners complained about the Muslim diet in the jail, he responded that "taste and delight" are not a faith requirement for their meals!

Khalil and I attended a training event for chaplains to address the issue of the "radicalisation" of Muslim prisoners while they were in prison. At one of these events, an older male probation officer spoke across the group in my direction, saying vaguely, "Don't you think that people living in our country should just accept our way of life?" I asked if he was speaking to me and said "I'm afraid I'm a foreign national! You'd better ask Khalil – he's the Englishman". Not only did that put an end to such nonsense, but it cemented a friendship with my Muslim colleague, which has lasted for 25 years.

As a footnote to the "diet" issue, I really must add that a few young offenders used to register on arrival as Mormon. This entitled them to a drink of hot chocolate in the evenings, to distinguish them from the "other" tea-drinkers. So "taste and delight" was not exclusive to Muslim prisoners!

In the Middle Ages, Islam brought much scholarship and enlightenment to the world. Without the Muslim translations of ancient texts, such as Aristotle's writings, the Western Renaissance and the Enlightenment could have been delayed for decades. Christianity more often attempted to restrict scientific awareness and development.

The Flat Earthers and Geo-centrists would not let Galileo away with any of his scientific assertions. In the Middle Ages, the church blocked scientific progress in geology, astronomy and biology. Today's creationists follow in this tradition by denying the benefit of Darwin's scientific research to the world, as though it were the work of the devil!

Islam and Christianity have in common an inheritance of male domination. I have engaged in many conversations with Muslim people – male and female – who dispute that. Yet the observations we can make, looking around the world, emphatically support this contention. In recent decades, we have seen some Christian churches promote the leadership of women at all levels. Boy/girl, what a struggle that has been!

But the whole ethos of these religions is masculine, in the service of a God who is male. These communities are not modelling inclusion and acceptance, despite their verbal attempts to suggest otherwise. How can you redesign the model when you refuse to accept that the basic assumptions are the problem?

All religions offer community – a place to belong. Hospitality is a core service of such fellowship. So many people need just that. Can you please reset your baselines to meet these travellers at the point of their need, instead of unquestioningly serving the (sometimes whimsical) demands of this awesome divine being? As communities, we have much to offer. Let us do so in a spirit of openness and willingness to learn.

Once, I was invited along with others to address a meeting in a Muslim community centre in Batley, West Yorkshire, to discuss how we might respond to "Radicalisation and Terrorism". The best I could suggest was that we should bring a terrorist home for tea! This is no joke. It is so important for those who are outside to feel that they are welcome, and that judgement can be set to one side to enable relationships to develop. All religions need to increase their community capacity for accepting people, and listening to their stories, and offering them tea and understanding.

And *Paganism,* yes Paganism! How did that slip in here – well, following the detention of Greenham Common women, and other eco-warriors, there were requests from prison inmates to have a visit from their Pagan "minister". I guess you are thinking "Druid priests" here? The reality is that there is quite an extensive network of Pagans around England, although it is sometimes difficult to recruit such a potential visitor due to distance.

There is a national coordinating body for pagans, which would locate someone in the general area. These visitors were delightful people – often Greens – who ideologically found prison an inappropriate way to deal with offending (as do many others). They provide reading material and advice around the celebrations of festivals, many of which coincide with "Christian" seasons (e.g., Christmas/Winter festival and Easter/Esther). The word "pagan" means "of the countryside". In that respect, readers of the New Testament could be tempted to think of Jesus as a pagan – given his rural journeys, his mountain sermon and lakeside preaching.

Are *Atheists* our brothers and sisters, or our enemies? People of no faith, or who state explicitly that they are atheists, have a vague recollection of his sympathetic smile as I sailed off into oblivion!

A groggy afternoon waking up back on St Peter's Ward – no, I had not arrived in heaven! I was delighted to have scrambled eggs on toast to break my fast. Did I notice that the ward sister was avoiding eye contact? Was I imagining that the "normal" chitchat between nurse and patient was missing from around my bed? Well, no, I wasn't. Around 5.30, they came, two of them, looking hesitant. One of them fumbled with the curtains, trying to get them closed around the bed. "Curtains, doctor?" I asked. They looked at each other, slightly embarrassed. The surgeon flushed slightly before telling me that the lump in my groin was not in fact a hernia, but a small tumour. They had sent it to the lab for testing and they would get back to me within 48 hours when the results came back. I was stunned.

I reported home by telephone and heard my wife Joss's gasp when I mentioned "tumour". I had by now given my head the idea that this had a 50-50 chance of being benign, so I would not jump the gun. Joss was not amused – nor was the consultant who arrived by my bed with a colleague on Wednesday morning. He informed me that the lump was indeed malignant, a word that certainly grabbed my attention – no metaphor here. I had Hodgkin's Disease, a disorder of the lymph system.

He said that without the proper treatment, I could not expect to live longer than 18 months to 2 years. I raised my voice to him asking who "the ****" he thought he was? Poor man! He did not expect that his priest-patient would resort to such foul language. It was an opportunity for my humanity to shine through! Sister Angela said she would phone my wife to let her know about the diagnosis – as well as my profane outburst. My

deserve equal respect and consideration as those of our own tradition – *not* an attempt to convert them – because they are human, and we all belong together. Do we speak to people of no faith with a lack of academic integrity, even a lack of spiritual authenticity? I have done so, on occasions, to my shame.

In Limerick, back in 1978, Davy Burns introduced me to some atheist reading material. I was amazed by the positivity of the writing and the sense of wonder and the celebration of life. He might have been one of the first self-professed atheists I had met. Jim Kemmy was another. I couldn't have had more respect for any human being than I have for these two men. Since the 1980s, I have, of course, met many others who have no God-faith, and I see none of these people lacking in any spiritual or moral strength.

They have weighed up their circumstances and life challenges and have come to different conclusions than we have. They are worth listening to, and they will appreciate the attention, just as any other person would. It should not really be necessary to call for respect for those who do not believe in a god. It diminishes people of faith when we feel justified in sidelining or denigrating the reasonable and personal beliefs of others.

Were the native Americans who performed rain dances for their crops, somehow inferior to us, spiritually? We might have laughed at such practices in the past, as though we are superior in some way. What I would like us to do is laugh at our own spiritual/religious practice. Send it up a bit. See what is silly, as silly. Stop taking it all as Gospel. Enjoy it.

And this brings me to the final point in this chapter – a familiar saying of Jesus: "First take the plank out of your own eye before you try to help remove the speck of dust from your brother's". There is a proper sense of humour in this – almost ridiculous. How could you possibly see *any*thing with a plank sticking out of one eye? The point is that none of us holds *the high moral ground*. That does not mean that there is no morality, but we do not have the right to apply it to others if we avoid it ourselves.

Our spirituality might be drawn towards the adulteress who was about to be stoned to death by some righteous Jews for her waywardness. First, the man who shared this encounter with her (the other adulterer) seems to have got off scot-free, and then Jesus tells the men of faith "Whichever one of you is sinless, go ahead and stone her" One by one the men walked away. "Where are they? Is there no one left to condemn you?" Jesus asks the woman. "No, sir, none." "Then neither do I", he says, advising her to go, and sin no more.

I do not say this to chide others, but to remind myself of how easy it is to adopt the high moral ground, which allows me to divert attention away from my own misdemeanours and focus on the weaknesses of others. Religious leaders are often the most vulnerable to adopting this stance, so you should be wary of them. It seems like Jesus certainly was when you read the words he allegedly used to call out the Pharisees and Sadducees.

> "I'm still an atheist, thank God!"
> – *LUIS BUÑUEL*

ENDNOTES

6   Fuengsin Trafford, born in Thailand, inherited from her Ajahn or teacher of the Buddha's path his handwritten book on advanced meditation practice. As a wife, mother and lay teacher in England, she fulfilled his prophecy that she would one day be an outstanding teacher of Buddhism herself. Remarkably, it was through her own contemplative experience and by learning to draw on many spiritual traditions and secular customs that she applied her training to help people from all walks of life.

Health and Healing – Death and Dying

The Healing experience – and the perception of what wholeness is.

> "If the rich could pay other people to die for them, the poor could make a wonderful living."
> – *YIDDISH PROVERB*

Many years ago, my GP discovered I had a lump in my groin and the diagnosis was "hernia". Because I was moving up-country, I decided to defer the operation for a while. By March, my new GP had arranged that I would go into the Mater Hospital on the evening of 18th April 1982, after fulfilling all my Easter commitments. There was little concern or alarm, and I was expected home within a few days, so no need for any of the family to travel from Cootehill to Dublin to visit me. Gordon Farrell, a parishioner and local businessman, very kindly drove me down and dropped me off.

The following morning – no breakfast, just a funny gown, pre-med, and off to theatre. I remember telling the anaesthetist that I would stay awake for the whole proceedings and deserve equal respect and consideration as those of our own tradition – *not* an attempt to convert them – because they are human, and we all belong together. Do we speak to people of no faith with a lack of academic integrity, even a lack of spiritual authenticity? I have done so, on occasions, to my shame.

In Limerick, back in 1978, Davy Burns introduced me to some atheist reading material. I was amazed by the positivity of the writing and the sense of wonder and the celebration of life. He might have been one of the first self-professed athe-ists I had met. Jim Kemmy was another. I couldn't have had more respect for any human being than I have for these two men. Since the 1980s, I have, of course, met many others who have no God-faith, and I see none of these people lacking in any spiritual or moral strength.

They have weighed up their circumstances and life challeng-es and have come to different conclusions than we have. They are worth listening to, and they will appreciate the attention, just as any other person would. It should not really be neces-sary to call for respect for those who do not believe in a god. It diminishes people of faith when we feel justified in sidelining or denigrating the reasonable and personal beliefs of others.

Were the native Americans who performed rain dances for their crops, somehow inferior to us, spiritually? We might have laughed at such practices in the past, as though we are superior in some way. What I would like us to do is laugh at our own spiritual/religious practice. Send it up a bit. See what is silly, as silly. Stop taking it all as Gospel. Enjoy it.

And this brings me to the final point in this chapter – a familiar saying of Jesus: "First take the plank out of your own eye before you try to help remove the speck of dust from your brother's". There is a proper sense of humour in this – almost ridiculous. How could you possibly see *anything* with a plank sticking out of one eye? The point is that none of us holds *the high moral ground*. That does not mean that there is no morality, but we do not have the right to apply it to others if we avoid it ourselves.

Our spirituality might be drawn towards the adulteress who was about to be stoned to death by some righteous Jews for her waywardness. First, the man who shared this encounter with her (the other adulterer) seems to have got off scot-free, and then Jesus tells the men of faith "Whichever one of you is sinless, go ahead and stone her" One by one the men walked away. "Where are they? Is there no one left to condemn you?" Jesus asks the woman. "No, sir, none." "Then neither do I", he says, advising her to go, and sin no more.

I do not say this to chide others, but to remind myself of how easy it is to adopt the high moral ground, which allows me to divert attention away from my own misdemeanours and focus on the weaknesses of others. Religious leaders are often the most vulnerable to adopting this stance, so you should be wary of them. It seems like Jesus certainly was when you read the words he allegedly used to call out the Pharisees and Sadducees.

> "I'm still an atheist, thank God!"
>
> – LUIS BUÑUEL

ENDNOTES
....

6   Fuengsin Trafford, born in Thailand, inherited from her Ajahn or teacher of the Buddha's path his handwritten book on advanced meditation practice. As a wife, mother and lay teacher in England, she fulfilled his prophecy that she would one day be an outstanding teacher of Buddhism herself. Remarkably, it was through her own contemplative experience and by learning to draw on many spiritual traditions and secular customs that she applied her training to help people from all walks of life.

—

Health and Healing –
Death and Dying

T he Healing experience – and the perception of what wholeness is.

> "If the rich could pay other people to
> die for them, the poor could make a
> wonderful living."
> – *YIDDISH PROVERB*

Many years ago, my GP discovered I had a lump in my groin and the diagnosis was "hernia". Because I was moving up-country, I decided to defer the operation for a while. By March, my new GP had arranged that I would go into the Mater Hospital on the evening of 18th April 1982, after fulfilling all my Easter commitments. There was little concern or alarm, and I was expected home within a few days, so no need for any of the family to travel from Cootehill to Dublin to visit me. Gordon Farrell, a parishioner and local businessman, very kindly drove me down and dropped me off.

The following morning – no breakfast, just a funny gown, pre-med, and off to theatre. I remember telling the anaesthetist that I would stay awake for the whole proceedings and have a vague recollection of his sympathetic smile as I sailed off into oblivion!

A groggy afternoon waking up back on St Peter's Ward – no, I had not arrived in heaven! I was delighted to have scrambled eggs on toast to break my fast. Did I notice that the ward sister was avoiding eye contact? Was I imagining that the "normal" chitchat between nurse and patient was missing from around my bed? Well, no, I wasn't. Around 5.30, they came, two of them, looking hesitant. One of them fumbled with the curtains, trying to get them closed around the bed. "Curtains, doctor?" I asked. They looked at each other, slightly embarrassed. The surgeon flushed slightly before telling me that the lump in my groin was not in fact a hernia, but a small tumour. They had sent it to the lab for testing and they would get back to me within 48 hours when the results came back. I was stunned.

I reported home by telephone and heard my wife Joss's gasp when I mentioned "tumour". I had by now given my head the idea that this had a 50-50 chance of being benign, so I would not jump the gun. Joss was not amused – nor was the consultant who arrived by my bed with a colleague on Wednesday morning. He informed me that the lump was indeed malignant, a word that certainly grabbed my attention – no metaphor here. I had Hodgkin's Disease, a disorder of the lymph system.

He said that without the proper treatment, I could not expect to live longer than 18 months to 2 years. I raised my voice to him asking who "the ****" he thought he was? Poor man! He did not expect that his priest-patient would resort to such foul language. It was an opportunity for my humanity to shine through! Sister Angela said she would phone my wife to let her know about the diagnosis – as well as my profane outburst. My better nature partially restored, I said "Thank you" to the two men. They left, seemingly with less anxiety than when they had arrived. As patients, we try to make it all right for the doctor to give us the worst possible news. Of course, it is not the doctor's fault – he or she is simply the messenger.

We might look further into this prognosis and the hospital experience at some later date, but for now I want to say how faith-less my response to this crisis was. After crying my eyes out and snapping at any nurses or other patients who tried to console me, I went into an unusual (for me) withdrawal. I wanted to deny the reality, and I considered asking for a "second opinion".

Then I told myself that this illness was well-deserved – for all my misbehaviour from childhood to the present. My unworthiness surfaced like a flood, reminding me of my catalogue of offending. Chiding myself with "should haves" further eroded my confidence. I felt like there was just an outer skin cloaking the emptiness that was me, and that these feelings were occurring in some other place altogether. Later I became angry with the church and a God who could ask me to give so much of myself to "divine" work – and this is what I get!

Then, I slept with utter exhaustion. I woke at about 2 am and thought I should talk to my dear friend, Brian Smeaton. He has been a very affirming support during much of my adult life, and I received from him reassurances that this new information was/is "completely undeserved". That made me cry again – alone, on a public phone at the end of a dark hospital corridor, in the middle of the night. He asked me to say it out loud: "This is totally undeserved", repeating it until he could sense that I had begun to believe it myself. He then told me he was going back to sleep, and he would talk to me soon again.

Kevin Dalton (Rev Kev) came to visit me on the ward before breakfast at 7. He could see I had been crying and told me I would find a way through. He was convincing. His chat was light and affirming and a relief from the heaviness I felt.

Frank Gleeson, a student from the University of Limerick, called in later that morning to the wrath of Sister Angela, who complained that it wasn't visiting time. When I suggested that I'd go downstairs to talk with him, she relented and let him stay. Frank was crucial to my next "moves". When he asked if there was anything he could do to help, I asked him if he could find out about this Hodgkin's Disease and let me know.

Within 24 hours, he brought back a treasure of info, a snippet of which I will share with you now. During World War I, several men who were suffering from Hodgkin's Disease were sent to fight at the front, where they were exposed to mustard gas. Those who did not die from the conflict returned home to discover that the symptoms of their disease had disappeared! Frank also provided me with the contact details of a Chinese Medicine practitioner and a homoeopath.

I called the Chinese guy somewhere in County Kilkenny. When an English-speaking voice eventually came on, I explained what I was looking for. Again, I was at the end of the corridor on the public phone, inserting pennies and shillings at a great rate. Following my statements, the voice was translating into Chinese, and I'd hear a distant voice respond. Then my "connection" would translate back to me. After 10 minutes – and about one pound fifteen shillings – he asked about the lump. I used the word "malignant" which he translated instantly, and I could actually *hear* the shake of the doctor's head as the line went dead! How empty could a body feel? At the end of a cold, dark, empty hospital corridor!

Kevin called again just after tea. He said he happened to be over this side of the city and just popped in. I knew he was lying – he came out of concern for me, and I felt incredibly supported. (In fact, he came to see me, at some point, every single day during that hospital stay; he even brought along with him, one Sunday, Lord Soper, an English Methodist minister, socialist and pacifist, after he had preached in Kevin's parish!) I was able to call home that night and spoke to one or two of the children and to Joss. The doctors were doing further tests, so I was now staying in over the weekend to await the results early the following week.

After my discharge from hospital, I was very active at home. I did not feel very much in charge of my life, but I worked on that and wrestled with whether it might not be easier just to give up and die. Being around the children, and fearing not seeing them grow up, became such a big factor to me. With the emotional distress of the past weeks, I was even more short-tempered than usual. This was a time when I really wanted them to know how much I loved them, but I could not seem to communicate that.

And then a letter arrived, offering an appointment for St Luke's Hospital in Rathgar – a Dublin suburb – to receive radiotherapy. We decided I should stay in Dublin from Monday to Friday each of the 6 weeks for my treatment. Freda Hogan, an excellent friend of our family, very kindly arranged an apartment where I could stay, nearby, within walking distance of St Luke's. This was a wonderful gift, as I really wasn't looking forward to spending all day, every day, in the company of other cancer patients. Dr Ogden provided me with some homoeopathic remedies to ameliorate the harsh effects of the radiation. I certainly didn't appear to suffer quite as much as some of the other patients I encountered in the waiting areas.

The Falklands War was happening at that time and I was bemused by the way the UK government orchestrated the press to ensure that this was seen as a righteous venture. There was a Dáil by-election in Dublin West, and on several evenings I caught the bus to do some canvassing for the Democratic Socialists. I was off alcohol at the insistence of my new homoeopath. I continued to smoke – but that too was to cease, as and when I could cope with such a life-change. Having a coffee in Rathmines, or occasionally in Bewley's on Grafton Street, was much preferable to the, albeit pleasant, surroundings of the hospital coffee shop. Being out and about was a way for me to start feeling "in charge" of myself, my journey and my destination.

Although I looked forward to weekends back home, I was often too tired to get the most out of the family time. I was sleeping relatively well at night *and* for quite a few hours during the day. I found it difficult to greet visitors from the town, who wanted only to wish me well and perhaps try to cheer me up. Just as with hospital visits, the patient is expected to make everyone else feel OK about how things are going – even when she/he is frightened and unsure.

"I am" the one enduring this life sentence.
"Where am I?" spiritually.
I am faithless – fearful
and
I am feeling loved – worthy – confused.

Cancer
slight
blight
on life.

I started back at work in August, feeling really positive. We had enjoyed a family holiday in Donegal. We played and sang and went to the cinema. Our home life was brightening up. Work was a welcome distraction from my preoccupation with illness. Lots of conversation still centred on my health, but I was generally quite upbeat about this. I found great encouragement from all the people in Cootehill – and a degree of interest in homoeopathy. I was slowly regaining my energy levels and willing gradually to take on my full work responsibility.

My bishop and fellow clergy were very supportive, and the people in the parishes were just amazing. My friends elsewhere, some of whom had assumed I was on my way to the knacker's yard 6 months before, reconnected and cheered me on. The drama had subsided, and ordinary living was most welcome.

And then, two months later, symptoms reappeared. In mid-November, I began to experience numbness in my feet. I said nothing to anyone at first – hoping, as men do, that it will pass in due course. By Christmas, I was dragging myself on crutches, having lost the power of both legs. I was fuming. This loss of mobility, and the prospect of further decline, led to a deep hopelessness I had never felt before. I lost any sense of my usual determination and slowly slid into despair and depression.

I had several short hospital stays back in Dublin. More tests were done – angiogram, CT scan, biopsy, bone marrow aspiration. One morning, I was invited across to St Vincent's Hospital, from the Mater, where my case was the focus of a lecture theatre full of medical students. After the surgeon had introduced my diagnosis, he foolishly asked if he had got everything right. "Mostly", I said with some gravity, "except that this is not Hodgkins' Disease, it's Tarleton's Disease –

it's *mine*." The ensuing laughter ended any semblance of seriousness, but I had, almost unconsciously, made a very significant point. Hodgkins was a medic who had identified the disease – he himself had not endured it.

Still, it was clear now that I had the disease in lymph nodes low down inside my spinal sheath. Their enlargement was pressing on the nerves and disabling my legs from functioning. My homoeopath was continuing to treat me, and I was still attending appointments with the haematologist. There was no improvement, neither was there any deterioration at this point. Then in Holy Week, 31st March 1983, Kathleen Eakin, a local friend, rang up to say that there was a Healing Service in Monaghan that evening. If I would like to go, she would take me. I declined, as I felt that there was little point.

Despite my refusal, Kathleen turned up soon after tea and insisted that I go with her. I made further excuses, but she finally had me when she said, "I will not stand by while your health deteriorates further – just come and give it a chance". Joanne, our older daughter, offered to accompany me, so I agreed to go. I was bundled, crutches and all, into the back of Kathleen's business vehicle, and off we went to Monaghan.

The speaker was a priest from the North, Cecil, with whom I had had quite a public dispute about the upcoming abortion referendum, so I was a little apprehensive about that. When we got to the part where ministers offered the Laying-on-of-hands to the sick, Joanne coaxed me out of the pew. As I pulled myself up on the crutches, I whispered to her, "Maybe I'll be throwing these away in a while!". It was the first moment of levity I'd experienced in months. As I knelt at the communion rails, I made a quiet prayer to the divine: "Please let it not be Cecil who comes to me". And, sure enough, it *was* Cecil! He looked at me and asked what I wished for my healing. I responded that I wished to be healed of my anxiety (where did that come from?).

We made it back to our seat, still using the crutches, yet I felt a smile on my face and saw one on Joanne's. Having her there with me at that moment was magical, and having a friend like Kathleen was a gift. Instead of moping, like on the journey to Monaghan, I had some conversation on the journey home. The following Wednesday I was due for an appointment in Dublin with the haematologist. On Monday, I thought I felt some twinges in my left leg. On Tuesday I thought I had some feeling on the right. Remember that at this stage I had had no feeling in either leg for four months.

Dr Brian Otridge, the haematologist, was patient as ever – I was the "*im*patient". He told me he was really concerned about my lack of progress and would soon insist that I go for chemotherapy. I pleaded with him to delay this for a short while because I had noticed some feeling in my legs. He then agreed to use his little rubber hammer to test my reflexes. There was a tiny response on each leg, but he cautioned that this could not be used to indicate change. He warned me that on the next visit in two weeks I should come prepared for further treatment – meaning chemotherapy.

My spirits were "up". I knew that my reflexes had been non-existent 4 months earlier. I had a sense that the homoeopathic remedies were working. I dragged my legs with more enthusiasm. I noticed each day that I had more balance when standing. One day my foot felt a tiny pebble in my shoe! Another day, Kevin, our youngest son, pinched me on the thigh – I felt that. So, when my next appointment came, I travelled with my crutches to Dublin, where my reflexes were tested once more. Dr Otridge knelt forward in front of me and tapped the knee with his "hammer". The reaction was so forceful that he was almost knocked over backwards. We laughed. He tested the other knee, careful this time to stand a bit to one side. Again, the response was powerful.

We were both relieved and thrilled that the sign of progress was now visible and measurable. At no point did this specialist say he believed in the treatment for which I had opted, yet he had put no barriers in the way. He had proved the consummate healer by trusting his patient. I had more blood tests, and although I was recovering, the medics used the term "in remission" to describe my condition. I continued to have 6-monthly reviews over the next five years to ensure that "it" wasn't coming back. I knew I had been healed!

Homoeopathy is a holistic process – physical and personal. It is treatment in the knowledge that many of our ailments come from within – bodily, emotionally and psychologically. It trusts that with "like" remedies, our bodies can be prompted to recover our health and reset our survival as whole human beings. Just as I benefitted from the remedies in my cancer recovery, and through the radiation therapy, so I have continued to prefer this mode of treatment over the past 40 years – dealing with COPD (breathing) and Atrial fibrillation (Heart arrhythmia).

Allopathic medicine (the usual GP route) is very effective at diagnosis and vital for many emergencies. Homoeopathic treatment is gentle and person-focussed. It offers some generic remedies which will alleviate certain conditions in most people, but with chronic complaints there is a need to explore the individual's overall state of health before deciding on remedies. There is the assurance that, whatever treatment I receive from a homoeopath, there will be no long-term side effects. Some people regard its success as "mind over matter", but animals also recover from disease through homoeopathic remedies – so that can hardly be the action of mental power.

To opt for this form of therapy is very much an individual choice – and not one to be decided by one person for another. Still, there is so much public scepticism and alarm over homoeopathy among allopathic practitioners that I wonder if they don't protest too much! The power of medicine sometimes mirrors the past power of the church – not to be contradicted or challenged.

Dr Elizabeth Ogden was a registered GP who decided after many years' practice to train in homoeopathy, and her work was very precise and focussed. During months of uncertainty around my healing, she exuded a confidence in the process, which sustained my recovery at a time when Joss's anxiety and the haematologist's concern were raising questions about my sanity. I would still allow for questions about my mental balance, but in this particular situation, my resolve was eventually rewarded.

When we pray, are we asking for miracles? Do we just fear change and loss? Loss may be... of life, of a limb, of mobility. Grief and bereavement can accompany any of these. A broken relationship can be just as devastating. When our spirit is challenged in a life-threatening situation, we are forced to acknowledge how vulnerable we are. The vagaries of life sometimes push us to the limits of our capacity to manage, to survive.

It is perhaps in this emptiness that there is a sense of a connection to a deeper or higher power. To attribute such depth and power to God is our traditional way of making sense of this. In homoeopathy, the remedy simply offers the body the stimulus to recover itself; to restore the Life Force. In our spirituality too, the awareness of our vulnerability awakens the I AM of the divine *within*, to prepare us for wherever the next stage of the journey leads.

Paradoxically, in spirit terms, it is this vulnerability which is the catalyst for accessing our strength. Trust or faith helps us allow what is going to happen to happen. Acceptance of the ebbing tide gives a corresponding expectation of its return in the fullness of time – whatever form that will take as the crisis unfolds.

To face the prospect of dying, at any age, is a daunting challenge. I have spent time with clergy at the end of their lives, and some have expressed disappointment at the poverty of the approaching end. Others have smiled their way into what they anticipated as "glory". One elderly priest could not understand why his undignified hospital bed departure should be his reward for a dedicated life of service to God. How could the almighty do this to me?

In the case of this man, I asked him what promises he had received in advance? He was startled into a look of agony, which after some minutes became a smile – even his eyes lit up. I simply reminded him that this is what he's got, and he makes of it what he can. Like a child, he asked what it would be like? Would he be welcome? So, I asked him what he hoped for. What would he like? He cried, saying he did not know. Having sat at the bedside of dying people himself on many occasions over the years, he was now shorn of any pretence about the promise of the eternal life of which he had assured others.

It was at this point that I offered some of the poetry by Khalil Gibran, author of *The Prophet*. As he absorbed each image, he reflected in silence, smiling with some sense of contentment. The tried and trusted Psalm 23, with its "walk through the valley of the shadow of death", was not meeting this man's need at this moment, but these words brought him the imagery and assurance his living spirit required:

For what is it to die but to stand naked in
the wind and to melt into the sun?
And what is it to cease breathing, but to
free the breath from its restless tides,
that it may rise and expand and seek God
unencumbered?

Only when you drink from the river of
silence shall you indeed sing.
And when you have reached the mountain
top, then you shall begin to climb.
And when the earth shall claim your
limbs, then shall you truly dance.

"Death" from *The Prophet* – KHALIL GIBRAN

CHAPTER 8

If You Meet the Buddha on the Road...

When you ask about spirituality, you are seldom recommended a book to read – or a person to visit – because most people have their own answer *for you* and their reply will be to state what it means *for them*! Underlining the subjective nature of this aspect of life, Sheldon Kopp wrote the book *If You Meet the Buddha on the Road, Kill him...* – quoting a famous ninth-century Zen Buddhist adage. I think he is warning us of self-professing Masters of Spirituality. There has traditionally been a notion of power attached to the teaching of spiritual issues. Kopp was a psychotherapist who warned people against looking to others for enlightenment – rather we should uncover the light wit*hin*.

Assumptions – Wilfred Bion was a British psychoanalyst who worked with traumatised war victims. He was also a proponent of group dynamics. He highlighted how basic assumptions guided the behaviour of groups. Such assumptions cannot be allowed to continue unchallenged in groups, to the point where we all agree that the naked king is fully clothed! The human need for a Messiah can overwhelm our collective capacity to find what we need within the elements (material and spiritual) of our own existence.

There is a human propensity to externalise the crisis and the resolution, to objectify rather than work internally. Anyone who intends to work in a community needs to understand how groups work. They need to understand that things go wrong, not because people are bad, but because the group fluctuates in and out of dysfunction. The leader will often be the butt for the dissatisfaction of the other participants. Religious leaders would do well to explore this dimension.

I have already mentioned how important and valuable it was for prisoners to be offered the attention of psychotherapists and counsellors. I also referred to how I availed of such therapy myself on an ongoing basis for my professional survival and personal development. I truly believe that such support should be available to anyone and everyone – in a low-key, matter-of-fact way. It should not be remarkable that everyone could benefit from an opportunity to review their lives and make sense of the dysfunction which is evident in all family and individual living.

Just think about it for a moment! You wouldn't stop for a second to make an appointment with the doctor if your temperature shoots up, or if you fall and break a bone. Yet we smile to hide deep emotional hurt, which we experience from time to time in relationships or disappointments or failures. All that untreated distress must go somewhere – usually internally. It often causes physical disease, as well as damage to our psyche. Our minds and our spirits deserve this attention. Why should we deny ourselves the relief and peace we desperately need?

The attention we receive through therapy need not be for a fixed period – it really could be part of our lifelong learning. We become empowered to review and evaluate our experiences as we live and grow. There is a particular discipline within this practice called Re-evaluation Co-counselling (RC). Brian and Sandra Smeaton have embraced me with their encouragement and support, especially when I have been up against it. They are active counsellors in the home and in the community. RC is democratic, and "equal". The newcomer receives no more attention than the experienced practitioner. The *process* is key. The boundaries and outcomes are the responsibility of the participants. Like other forms of counselling, it is completely confidential – and it is *free*!

Even when we receive attention from an experienced counsellor, we are, each one of us, Master of our own destiny. The idea that there is a person – out there – appointed to take care of another's spirit denies the responsibility we each have for our own being. So, *no* Masters! Perhaps you will find some fellow travellers more helpful on your journey than others. That's a matter for you to decide. But we must refrain from the cult, which elevates some over others. Hierarchical religious institutions cannot help themselves – it's in their DNA to remain absolute and unchangeable! They need to die or change dramatically.

Ivan D Illich, best remembered for *Deschooling Society*, and many other helpful books on the nature of institutions, presented his "Negative Design Criteria" to a group in Ireland in the mid-1980s. Paddy Doherty from Derry's Bogside was present. He found it a helpful way to analyse any institution, including the one he was operating at the time – the Derry Youth and Community Workshops. The "Criteria" would suggest that organisations naturally go "off-key" after a certain period of existence. Then they really need to start all over again.

Paddy believed that "welfare" for young unemployed people was devaluing their worth and denying them the opportunity to grow and develop their leadership capacity. Few

Derry teenagers would have had the chance – or the desire! – to take part in the Duke of Edinburgh's Award scheme. However, the outward-bound training and the personal and group survival challenges involved in this scheme *do* generate skills for life. Paddy envisioned and created a programme where young people could take part in an active community and increase the awareness of their talents and strengths.

None of this could happen within a hierarchical framework, where managers defend their status and power. Doherty thought outside the box big-time, and the Community Workshops became a new model for young people to find their level in society, without the debilitating label of being "welfare recipients".

Negative Design Criteria[7] – to be applied to Organisations

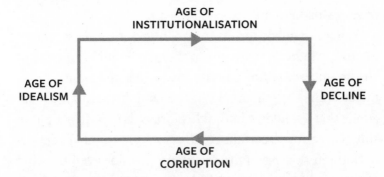

From the bottom left-hand corner there emerges an idea, which, when shared, generates an exciting ideal that encourages people to DO something, perhaps in response to a community challenge. (A of Id)

As the idea becomes concrete and a project gets off the ground, it becomes necessary to tie down the ideals and make the project workable, and the workers accountable to the plan. (A of In)

Now that the project is functioning, there is an assumption that all is well. Workers' rights/needs, and leaders' career paths become significant, and the idea at the core of the organisation becomes moderately marginalised. (A of D)

Leaders realise that there is a conflict between the origins of the project and its need to keep going (survival). They now require that the idealism upon which the whole thing was founded has to be subverted or corrupted to keep the show on the road. (A of C)

* * *

I have worked in schools, universities, hospitals, prisons and in the church. This model applies equally to any or all of them. Do you recognise some of these stages in some aspects of your work and life?

Being ordained a priest in 1974 was not for me a following in my father's footsteps, rather a personal response to all the uncertainty of a faith that had been drummed into me at home, in school and in the church (parish). I must admit that I couldn't have felt more at home than a pig in shit. There was a certain comfort in knowing that there is nothing in this system to frighten me – not even the God of the Old Testament, nor bishops, nor archdeacons. I was free to have fun, but I want to make clear, it wasn't a game. It has been, and still is, a journey into wisdom that I hope will continue until my dying day.

I never wanted to become a guru – yet I received invitations from some people to fulfil that role for *them*. It's very flattering to the ego when asked to lead someone else's life. And many clergy and other faith leaders have been tempted to go down that road. It is unhealthy for the "client" (parishioner/inmate/patient/staff) and very inappropriate for the "professional". Who do we think we are? We have no right to determine for others what they should do in the most trying situations of their lives. Whether it is a request for help with a pregnancy termination, or to attend *Dignitas* with them, to assist in their wish to end their life.

As I was "growing up" in Northern Ireland, religion was a serious business. Spirituality was just an alternative word for religion. Even then, it was obvious to me that we had an issue with growing spiritually. When the well of your religious community is dry, and no longer reaches down into the river of Life – from which all spirit is nourished – then you're seriously lost. The "NO" of Ulster Protestantism appears to come from a deep, dark well of fear of the present. The only meaningful way to express our faith has been to act like our forefathers – yesterday's people; past, but not gone.

The Buddha in Northern Ireland is the Orange leader who insists that it is our duty to be led by our ancestors, as though they got everything right in their day. Who, then, will permit people to make their own mistakes in the present? Not the Orange Buddha, but *we ourselves* (coincidentally, the English translation of Sinn Féin). Since the institutions of power are inherited structures and resistant to challenge or change, then our spirituality will develop healthily only outside of these constraints.

So, at some point we must make a self-declaration:

I refuse to have my spirit dictated to by any
agency which is not committed fully to the

115

present time,
and I will offer all my support and encour-
agement to anyone else who is willing to risk
walking on this water with me!

I have to add here that I have encountered many courageous and inspiring people in Northern Ireland who have stepped out of line to discover a new harmony among their peoples. Gordon Wilson is one of them. His daughter Marie was killed in the Enniskillen bomb in 1987. Ivan Cooper, a Civil Rights leader, was another, and Willie Dickson, Colonel of the Ulster Defence Regiment; Eamon McCann, writer; Dermie McClenaghan, Socialist; Rev Ray Davey of the Corrymeela Community; Gerry Fitt, politician.

While the late John Hume rightly got great credit for leading his people into the new power-sharing deal, he was taking them in the direction they wanted to go. David Trimble had the tougher task, I think – taking his people in the direction they did *not* wish to travel. It was like the dismantling of South African apartheid – Nelson Mandela was leading where his followers had chosen. F W de Klerk was taking white South Africans in the opposite direction to their dream.

If we stand tall, it is because we stand on the shoulders of many ancestors (*African proverb*) and *not* in their shadow. This is our time. We must step up to the front line and exercise our authority. Despite the horrors of conflict and war, the spirit of peace and the desire to find resolution are never completely extinguished. Water flows in desert places. Each morning brings the gift of a new day.

Reviewing my own life, I can sense that the splitting between good and bad was probably the most destructive element in my early education and learning. Now I understand that to objectify all the good I sense as the person of God and all the bad as the devil, is a way of avoiding personal responsibility. I know many people of faith who have not felt oppressed by this pattern – but for me, it damaged and distorted my reality. It forged a judgementalism that endures to the present, and which I do my best to curb. We so easily learn to chide ourselves for our mistakes, when all we need for our personal growth is to acknowledge and learn from them.

The psychological effect of training young people into such patterns is to cause needless distress in human lives, which are emerging into the light or darkness of their own particular circumstances. I cannot underscore enough how much damage has been done to faithful people by that Doctrine of Original Sin over many centuries. It was conceived by a man who seems to have pushed his own wayward lifestyle to the limits – one St Augustine.

"It's only a sin if you *don't* enjoy it!"
– *RIOGHNACH CASEY*

ENDNOTES

7. Negative Design Criteria. The Ivan Illich matrix for reviewing the stages of institutional development (written for me on the back of an envelope by Paddy Doherty!)

—

CHAPTER 9

The Power of Fasting, Prayer and Silence

Fasting

Fasting is a long-established practice in many faith traditions, formalised into certain days and seasons so that there is a sense of community participation – Lent and Ramadan are the most notable of these. The story of Jesus of Nazareth's 40 days and 40 nights in the wilderness, before the start of his teaching work, prompts us to regard fasting as integral to the Christian faith journey. We have gone a bit "soft" on fasting since the 1960s, but the value of the practice should not be sidelined.

We eat too much, too often; our bodies are overloaded with food. Much of this food is processed and, to varying degrees, indigestible. It causes us to suffer from a catalogue of modern illnesses. Fasting allows us to give our digestive systems a break, while, at the same time, increasing our inner space. Consequently, this allows our perceptive and intuitive senses to grow.

Wisdom may not burst to the surface because you skip a meal or two, but the discipline of bringing your physical system under fresh direction creates the circumstances in which human understanding and compassion grow. This is a way in which you may *take charge* of your life.

To take a day out from food every month is not too great a challenge for most of us. An occasional 3-day fast – maybe twice a year – will deepen the experience. I usually allow myself to drink water, hot or cold, during any fast of over 24 hours. Others would say that's not really a fast, but it suits me.

Interestingly, when you develop the confidence to go an extra day beyond the 3, you may find a certain sense of "tripping" in which your level of perception can become heightened. It can be frightening by day 3 to realise that you are not hungry and that you could easily extend the commitment by another day. Don't do that. Stick to the plan you made so you and others around you can be clear about your intentions. Please note! Fasting is not an exercise in losing weight.

Some doctors and other health professionals may disapprove of the practice of fasting, so you must make this a personal decision and ensure that going without food for the duration will not be harmful to your health. Personally, I wish that those same doctors were as disapproving when it comes to the diet of many of their patients. But then doctors don't really cover diet significantly in their 6-year training. Obesity could be resolved by refusing licences to fast-food outlets to operate. However, we live in a "free"-market economy, in which big pharmaceutical companies are making their profits off *dis*ease, rather than health. Could they possibly have an investment in fast-food proliferation?

I feel a degree of discomfort when talking about fasting. My inherited understanding of this practice is that it is something to be done in secret, and not to be shouted about from rooftops! Well, as I became familiar with the month of Ramadan while working in prisons, it is clear that Muslims love to let the world know about their commitment to fasting. So I am less secretive than I used to be – even if I am still reluctant to say to friends that I can't meet them for lunch on a Friday because I'm fasting. However, if the invitation is sufficiently appealing, I can always be tempted to shift the fast to the following day!

The Ramadan fast is from dawn to sundown. But it is total – no food and no drink, even no smoking. However, after sunset, the daily fast is usually broken by eating dates, followed by what in most households would be a "feast". There is an opportunity for a pre-dawn meal to anticipate the coming hardship. I have observed that this religious practice is particularly challenging in the summer months. As the date for the celebration of Ramadan moves by about 12 days every year, I cannot imagine what it must be like in Saudi Arabian or Dubai heat – not allowing oneself even a drink of water.

Having a community fast in this way is sociable – and mutually supportive. Many Muslims donate alms to the needs of oppressed people, especially, I have noticed, during Ramadan. I've already mentioned the restaurant in Perth WA, where everyone may eat, and those who can afford to do so pay. By eating, or fasting, we can support those who have too little to nourish them. Maybe, if you belong to a group of people who enjoy challenges, you might fast *together* in a mutually encouraging way, and look at it as another aspect of health promotion!

I was always amused in Ireland that Friday was a "fast" day. We ate only fish – as though it was not actual food! For me, having fish was something to look forward to on Fridays – a treat. Red meat was regarded as the flesh of warm-blooded, land-based beasts. By exploiting this technicality with the skill of a Pharisee, people began consuming the flesh of fish in place of the flesh of animals on fast days. Eating fish on Fridays became a tradition among Catholics. I was later given a more prosaic reason – it was to ensure the survival of the Irish fishing industry!

I can't really talk here about fasting without also mentioning *what we eat*! I am forever grateful to Ann Lynch and Sheena Burns for introducing me to the macrobiotic diet. While it was a culinary challenge for me, it is also enriching, nutritious and holistic. Back in 1978, I remember attending a lazy weekend symposium on "Better Living" being held in Limerick. At the symposium, I was introduced to wonderful nut roasts and tasty salads peppered with pulses. It was in Ann's shared house near the Treaty Stone.

When I was being treated for my illness in 1982, my homoeopath insisted I become a vegetarian – and I followed her advice for the next 17 years, exploring an extensive range of wholesome non-meat dishes. Today we are more aware than ever of the impact of our food choices on the environment, as much as on our own bodies. Let our spiritual growth take into account the food needs of the whole human family around the planet. Consider how to meet our own requirements in balance with the needs of the Earth. Giving our bodies the very best nutrition will ensure that we optimise the benefits of our existence.

Prayer

All faiths have prayer at their core. Orthodox churches have liturgies of planned, programmed worship, in which intercessions and thanksgivings usually play a part. Much of the prayer is repetition, in that the same forms are used week after week. However, in the past thirty years, those prayers have become more "flexible" and easily identifiable with current national or world issues. Fr Michel Quoist was a wonderful innovator of reflective prayer in the 1960s. His meditative prayers focussed on: a man whose wife had just left him; a pornographic magazine; a drunk in the street – real-life issues.

Free churches often give the appearance of allowing the spirit to direct the words of the speaker – the preacher or those praying aloud for the community. If you listen carefully, there is a set pattern to much of this language too – it is not quite so "free" as you might expect. Certainly, these churches avoid dramatic rituals and dressing up, and in that sense they are free of some of the traditional practices.

Prayer time in worship can often be an important focus for a community, as it responds collectively to a crisis in a neighbouring family or the death of a well-known local person. Such expression helps to express the sum of the feelings of support and encouragement the church community wants for the families concerned. Sometimes very familiar prayers, said collectively, can be decidedly reassuring and comforting. I think that the context is as important as the words uttered. The deepest desires of the community, for the best outcome, penetrate the pain and loss, to access that spiritual realm where humans can feel relieved of their anxiety and distress.

Prayer has its greatest impact in two other settings: on my own, as I hold up the family, and the community I come from, daily. This is giving mindful attention to the people I care about and giving them the best spiritual support I can without being present with them. The other setting is in the intimacy of two or three people who wish to give thanks for something special – or who are experiencing a time of crisis. In these low-key expressions of prayer, there is a sense of reality and connection; no need to play to the gallery.

Prayer used with the Laying-on-of-hands is an identification with the healing ministry of Jesus. The physical touching – of the hands upon the head – can be emotionally moving and a dynamic experience. People attend healing services because of their own illnesses, or on behalf of friends or relatives. It is another form of spiritual uplifting. This is very much a lay ministry in the church – and is exercised collaboratively rather than by individuals.

Silence

I use the word "power" to express the impact of silence – not only in communal worship, but in personal life, and in relationships. Some silence can be filled with feeling – like fury, or sadness, for instance. But even that silence has *power*.

It wasn't only because of silence that I was attracted to the Society of Friends (Quakers). I had always admired their commitment since the nineteenth century to improving prison conditions in England – Elizabeth Fry being perhaps the most memorable of these campaigners. There is a non-judgemental element in Quaker life that respects people for their goodness, rather than for what they have done wrong. "Recognising that of God in everyone" is a central tenet of faith with this Society.

When I joined up in 1990, I found them to be remarkably inclusive. I enjoyed the silent Sunday meetings, which I was able to attend following my worship earlier in the prison chapel. The influence of the silence permeated how we arranged the services in the chaplaincy – generating more opportunity for reflection. Occasionally, Friends would come in on a Wednesday evening to lead a "meeting for worship" with the usual group. Just to reassure you that this was not to everyone's taste. One Wednesday evening in the chapel, after only two minutes of silence, one inmate roared aloud, "Speak, someone, for Christ's sake, I can't stand all this silence!".

Silence is a place where we may hear what is expressed, or withheld, without interruption or correction. It may offer a safe context for people to trust each other and share some of the depth of their emotions. It is a necessary corollary to listening – where people can begin to understand the meaning of some of their life crises. Often these do not need to be expressed in words – they form in the mind and are carried away with relief.

Promoting silence is also healthy. Again, we normally choose to find our quiet space or silent moments as individuals. It is possible to share silence, not just in a Quaker group, or at a counselling session, but with one or two other people who share our need for these moments. By setting the time and the location, we can make space in our lives for so much more than the necessary rough and tumble of daily living.

From a pastoral perspective, sometimes silence, more than words, is appropriate for a patient's needs. Let me tell you about a lovely lady, Anna, whom I visited several times in Cork city soon after I was ordained. She was extremely ill and close to dying. On the second visit, I prompted a brief conversation. Then I sat silently for less than a minute at her bedside. I leaned closer and asked:

"Would you like me to say a prayer with you?" She had obviously detected my discomfort.

"Well, if it helps you to feel more comfortable", she replied, with a hint of a smile at the edge of her lips! Thank you, Anna, for that lesson.

Contemplative groups which promote meditation are a sociable antidote to busy-ness. Our heads are chokka with panic about the latest thing we've forgotten, or the emails we need to write, or phone calls to answer. How can our spirituality flourish in such a stressful lifestyle? The answer is that it does! We grow through the distress, and our lives are enhanced by the skills and talents we uncover to manage our lives. It's the need to *balance* this that directs us towards fasting and silence.

For many people, even a good night's sleep would be refreshing. Well, why do we not sleep better? At the beginning of the 1900s, humans slept on average 9 hours per night. By the 1970s, this had reduced to 7 hours. Often, this is because we do not manage our stress. The unresolved issues of yesterday, and the anxieties about tomorrow's agenda, are rattling around so loudly in our subconscious that we simply don't relax into a deep sleep. Taking pills to address a problem that is potentially within our own capability to resolve is only a short-term solution. We need to better manage the use of electronic phones and televisions in the bedroom. You are in charge of your sleep – make sure you get it!

> "We cannot leave the haphazard to
> chance."
> – *N F SIMPSON*

CHAPTER 10

—

Hospitals and Hospices

It is a privilege to work in a hospital setting, among people dedicated to the care and well-being of those who arrive to receive treatment. The National Health Service is a remarkable organisation – it is the largest employer in Europe, with over 1.3 million employees and the world's biggest single employer of healthcare professionals. The people who (usually) smile at you as you walk along the corridors are very well trained and deeply committed to delivering a top-quality service to thousands of patients daily. The work is centred on the needs of many very vulnerable people. One reason for the NHS' ability to function so well is that many of its leaders are (and historically have been) women.

I guess that my own experience of a challenging diagnosis in hospital gave me a measure of understanding and empathy, which allowed me to function emotionally in such a culture. From the chaplaincy perspective, it was a case of dropping our religious denominational agenda and engaging the agenda of the hospital community. We do not *know* what patients need unless we ask them. Fortunately, our lead chaplain was focused on patient needs rather than church priorities. Not all members of the team were willing to share that agenda wholeheartedly.

As a chaplain in this setting, it is most likely that the expectations will be mostly religious – some people wanting to receive Holy Communion; anxious new parents wishing to have their newborn child baptised, to forestall the crisis which is facing them; people wanting to hear a reassuring prayer before an operation. Often, such requests come through the nursing staff on the wards.

I discovered that ward staff often had a preconceived notion of what a chaplain would do, so they tried to avoid the necessity of calling upon our services for fear of upsetting patients. However, I insinuated myself into the community of the wards to which I was appointed. I clarified that my role was to support and encourage staff, just as much as patients. I understood that the work of "Spiritual Care" is a joint venture for which *all* staff have a responsibility.

So, from time to time, I found slots during the working day when I could get 3 or 4 nurses together for 20 minutes to explore how we could deliver this spiritual care together. I have to preface this by saying that I am not an expert. I am a facilitator. Having had lots of experience of death and dying over the years, there was no longer anything that could phase me. Not even a late-night call-in to A&E, following a multi-car accident with lots of blood and guts, caused me to shrink from my work.

I'm not saying that at last I was ready to become a medic! It's just that the reason for my being there was clearly to support distressed relatives and stressed-out staff. Occasionally, when a group of newly-trained nurses came to work at our hospital, I'd have the chance to meet with them and let them know where we fitted into the hospital. And, when generic training was being provided, I would register so that I could take part in multi-disciplinary sessions.

This paid off in that invitations to spend time on wards increased and partnership working with other staff became the norm. The highlight of my collaborative work was when I was asked to dress up as a patient (attached to a drip) and talk to trainee staff about what I would expect from them. During my time in the NHS, there was a growing movement to involve ex-patients in advising how to improve the services offered.

When I wasn't attending wards, I spent a lot of time in other areas of the hospital – the admin department, the X-ray and scanning department, and the porters' tearoom. I observed a lot of the roles performed by many staff, and I came to a shocking conclusion. The best spiritual care in our hospital was being offered by the cleaners and the porters. This was upsetting for some chaplaincy staff, who rather thought that this was underplaying our area of expertise.

Most nursing staff could instantly see how valid my proposition was, but some chaplains just thought I was off the wall. When I explain, you will understand. Cleaners work around a patient's bed for a limited amount of time and they do not offer eye contact. Patients trust them with comments about their condition, and about their families, which they would not wish to have included in their medical file. These encounters are non-judgemental, and the confidences are shared outside of the clinical domain. Porters take anxious patients to appointments with consultants, or for minor surgical procedures. The patient, in a wheelchair, is facing away from the "driver" and chatters on about lots of issues of concern which they would never share with a priest. Again, completely confidential and non-judgemental.

Should we then offer these staff specialist training to enhance their spiritual skills? I really don't think so. I believe that the carefree attention they give to patients has great value in the hospital setting. The best way to move this issue

forward is to be more inclusive of them in our inter-disci-
plinary care, so that cleaners and porters feel appreciated for
the service they provide and for the role they play simply by
being themselves. That should not need to be said – but I'm
afraid that human snobbery still presumes certain roles are
less valuable than others.

Maternity was the busiest department, yet those staff who
wished to be trained to perform a baptism in an emergency
found the time. It wasn't a very demanding "course", and it
gave nurses a sense that, even if they were not particularly
religious, they could meet a mother's/family's urgent spiritual need in a crisis, rather than having to await the arrival
of a priest. In truth, *anyone* may baptise another person. Few
people know that.

One day, I was called by one of the gynaecological wards
to come and visit Judy. She was middle-aged and had received chemo treatment for a gynaecological problem two
years previously. She was in a single bed unit and was quite
distressed to hear news of a relapse. She was quiet, but not
shy. She told me she'd asked a nurse if there was a chaplain
who wasn't too religious and, oddly enough, my name came
up. This was not one of my duty wards, so I had to clear my
visit with the dedicated chaplain.

Over the next few days, and several quiet bedside visits,
she shared her story. After three days, she received further
news that her prognosis was now more critical – she was
very unwell. She wanted me to be with her when she told
the consultant that she had decided she would not have further chemotherapy. When he had gone, she asked me to remain. She was very open and, despite looking exhausted, she
shared more of her life crisis with me. I could see she was tir-
ing quickly, so I said I would pop in later before going home.

But with one last effort before she let me leave, she asked me if I would contact *Dignitas*[8] and get information for her about how she might end her life.

Judy was asleep when I called that evening. Although she had asked to be wakened if I arrived, the nurse and I agreed that she probably needed her sleep more than my visit. I made a commitment to return very early the following morning. Having slept on the issue of *Dignitas*, I felt quite at ease sitting down by her bedside. She had slept through the night and looked much stronger.

"Will you accompany me to Switzerland if we can make the arrangements?"

"Yes," I said, "if that is what you wish."

She accepted the photocopied pages on *Dignitas*, which I had downloaded the previous evening, and talked about her fears if she became unable to make decisions. I asked if she had left any documents with her lawyer to ensure that her wishes were respected by the hospital. She had.

At Judy's invitation, I shared a light breakfast in her room with her. She began to show a certain lightness of mood and fresh energy. She was almost playful, as though she had shrugged off all that fear, and was now completely in the present. She took my hand and held it for some time, before asking me to say a prayer for her in the chapel. Then she thanked me and said "Goodbye".

I accepted that our connection was over. She had decided not to go to Switzerland. It had been enough for her to hear only that I *would* accompany her. But exactly what that meant, I had no idea until four days later when I was called back by one of the nurses. Judy had passed away a few minutes earlier. She had refused all medication and food from the time of our shared breakfast. I was devastated but at the same time delighted for her that she had completed her intention in the best way she could under the circumstances. What a gift it was for me to have been invited into her crisis to share her spiritual journey, even for those few days. Over 10 years later, I still feel deeply moved by the memory of her courage and clarity.

Hospice

The hospice movement was a genuine attempt to provide a setting in which people could die with dignity and in comfort. It was designed to ensure that each patient would have the physical, emotional and spiritual support they needed as they approached the end of their lives. It is envisaged as the best model for "easing" people out of their physical life. However, the logistics of having these small units of perhaps up to 20 beds, with high-ratio staffing, would never meet the likely demand.

Research among patients consistently shows that the preferred place to die is at home. This has led to an increase in palliative care community nursing, perhaps most notably by the McMillan charity. With the best will in the world, and the need for beds to become available, hospice care can provide for only a small minority of the demand. Many people approaching the end of life require ongoing hospital interventions so that the timescale for transfer to home before death is often not possible.

The response to this has been to provide increased capacity *within* hospitals for end-of-life care and support in the interests of patients and their families. This latter development seems to be the completion of the "jigsaw". Hospices identified the need for specialised palliative care. Community nurses were engaged to work with those at home awaiting a hospice place.

Then the hospitals began to provide specialised services for those who could not be transferred to home or hospice.

Jean Roche ran the Education department at St Luke's Hospice in Sheffield. From time to time they very kindly invited me to share in the education programme for staff and volunteers. During those sessions – focussing upon the "Spiritual Care of the Dying" – we unpeeled the onion of our vulnerable selves and spoke out loud about some of the pain each of us had experienced. Without this self-understanding, much of the work with vulnerable patients/residents carries limited credibility. One question which I used to pose to volunteers was: "What's in this for you?" So many of the professionals and volunteers believed their motivation to be entirely selfless. This is seldom the case; we all have some agenda.

All the nursing staff I met and worked with in this sector were quite amazing. The demands of building relationships with people who are approaching their death are quite challenging. These nurses, almost all female, are exceptional human beings. Their employers need to recognise that such appointments could be time-limited so that post-holders don't experience burn-out. These staff should be given adequate emotional/psychological support to enable them to have a balanced life outside of their work location.

The one hesitation I have with the palliative concept is the area of pain control. While the patient is still conscious, she should be the one to determine how much pain management is required. She should indicate how this may continue once she loses consciousness. Patients and families need full information on how increased opiate interventions can cause organ damage and lead to a speedier decline.

Some people can manage a lot more pain than those around them, watching. Experiencing one's own death with clarity, rather than in a drug-induced stupor, may be for some the most fulfilling way to end their life. While these decisions are tough, the right of choice should be paramount – both for the patient's dignity and for her spiritual experience.

* * *

More recently, while working as a part-time chaplain to a HSE hospital in Ireland, I could sense that clergy of all denominations regard it as their *right* to visit people of their faith communities. This is not (or should not be) how it works. The hospital management has a responsibility to the patients to provide the spiritual care they need. They will engage whatever individuals and communities are best equipped to deliver that service. There is definitely a clash of priorities here, and the churches will have to adapt to the Healthcare policies. Watch this space.

In Ireland, the HSE (Health Service Executive) handles many of the roles that the churches had previously fulfilled – including the recording of Births, Marriages and Deaths. The Child Protection Agency, Tusla, also comes under their control. I know some of the healthcare managers, and they are extremely dedicated to their work. The government needs to recognise that much of what went wrong in the past was because the church operated a totalitarian system. Now, the danger is that the HSE is growing large and unwieldy and is beginning to operate in a totalitarian way itself. Everything is done in the best interests of all people, yet apparently incapable, at times, of meeting the needs of one particular person.

This is one reason spiritual care needs to be an integral part of the medical establishment. Health professionals are fully aware of the limitations of their services. They need help to understand that ongoing illnesses and deaths are not failures. The public must stop expecting the GPs and hospitals to lengthen our lives. There are other dimensions to our existence than simply being a functioning organism. Relationships provide us with opportunities to forgive and be forgiven as part of our recovery. Feeling the close presence of someone who can be trusted is an important aspect of healing that easily gets overlooked within institutionalised medical care.

On the relationship between the churches and the health service, my observation is that many people have let go of the notion of "eternal life" as offered by their religion. Now they almost expect that the HSE must provide them with a perpetual physical existence! We must understand that when such unreal expectations are foisted upon the medical establishment, failure will follow. But some medics will revel, like some clergy of the past, in their pseudo-messianic status; their control over other people's lives. Beware.

CHAPTER 11

—

Rainbows and Windmills

At school, I wasn't really over-interested in science. I remember how one afternoon I got a clip on the ear from our teacher in second-year chemistry. When he had passed around a glass tube with ammonia in it, I commented that it smelled just like pig shit. Of course, it was the ensuing laughter that caused the chastisement. Next chemistry class, I brought in an old syrup tin containing... pig shit. I wanted to make my point, but we reverted to the academic level quickly after that diversion!

I'm afraid that biology lost one of its potential Nobel laureates, the day Doc Simpson produced a tray of sheep's blood from the lab fridge. It was our Tuesday afternoon double-Biology class, and the moment he ran his fingers through the blood and stirred it around, I suddenly felt nauseous. I went all dizzy and fainted and fell off my stool onto the floor!

It was that religious blood again – the blood of the Lamb of God – and this time I hadn't the strength to run away. We guessed that "the Doc" maintained his capacity to function in a school community by availing of neat alcohol. This was located on the shelf next to his study door, and its purpose was to pickle any "interesting species" which might surface in the wetlands of County Fermanagh.

Where I did find some stimulation, however, was in the study of physics – electricity fascinated me. Light was a source of constant attraction to me. When we passed light through a prism to create a rainbow, I was thrilled. When we weighed different materials and designed scales to find balance, I was completely absorbed. The physics teacher wasn't particularly memorable, but the syllabus impinged positively upon my world.

Windmills

Windmills can be phantoms, which threaten some people's security. They are giants to be "tilted at" as in *Don Quixote*, and by me! They are also there to harness power to create energy and drive machinery. In my child's mind, I hold on to the notion of a personal windmill within everyone's life, converting the breath into energy for work and play – a generator driving the various elements of our existence, which, in harmony, portray the uniquely delightful human being each one of us is.

This is the personal portion of the "qi", the vital life force which ties together all the elements of the universe, according to classical Chinese Philosophy. It is a paradox because it is everything *and* nothing. You are your own windmill, and you will come to understand that, once you have taken charge of the events which relate to your life. I AM the driving force in my life. I am the wind; I am the sails.

Tvind

In July 1978, on my way to visit the World University near Thy in Denmark, I called to Tvind Folk Travelling High School. Here is a model of participative education in which the young people themselves devise their own curriculum. They engage the assistance of adult teachers and facilitators, in order to develop cooperatively according to their ability and ambition. Part of this development is to engage in real-life change in the surrounding community. Academic learning is useful for resource information and history. And there's an expectation of some practical application at the end, to evidence the impact of their "studies".

In 1973, due to the "oil crisis", there was a fear that the school might have to close. Several students, along with specialists, decided to do some research to explore what alternative possibilities existed for the future of the school. They discovered from local history that electricity-generating windmills had been a feature of that part of the Danish coast as far back as the 1870s. They researched different types of current windmills that could be used to produce electricity for their school needs. They visited successful operations of this type in several other countries.

They studied the relationship between supply and demand, so they would know how large their windmill needed to be. They estimated that, based on electricity usage in the school up to 1973, their generator should have a significantly greater capacity to allow for increased activity on the campus in the years ahead. Little did they imagine that the output would far exceed their needs and contribute to the local grid.

Eventually, they opted for the modern aeroplane-type propeller and costed the building of the large pillar necessary to support it. 600,000 Danish Crowns was the challenging figure (about €80,000 today). With parent support and school trustee commitment, they were granted a loan from a local bank, on the understanding that the savings made from the generation of this electricity would enable the repayment of the loan in 10 to 12 years.

By the time the windmill was up and running, I understand that the "debt" was due to be repaid at the end of only

6 years, because of the success of their innovative work. The educational content of their project included: economics, geography, history, physics, mathematics, organisation and community studies. I was convinced then about the need to develop alternative energy *and* for reviewing our educational models back home! Some months later, I was a member of a small group of Education students from Limerick to discover some of this Tvind model operating *live* in the Derry Youth & Community Workshops, already mentioned in Chapter 8.

At the World University near Thy, Aage Rosendal Nielsen welcomed me for a few days to wallow in the folk culture of the area. The small international community created a forum for lots of discussion about learning and education. On two separate evenings we walked two kilometres and back to an old school which was used for the narrating of "Folk Tales".

The programme was completely in Danish, but I listened avidly. My mind conjured up interesting tales as I felt the almost musical dialect wash over me. I checked with Aage later to see if the stories of my imagination had any correspondence at all to the tales we had heard – absolutely none! When the stories were over, we sang a Danish folk song one evening. I remember the simple air to this day. Perhaps someday I will write one of my imagined tales into a song, making use of that tune?

Windmills and power

By standing on a pier, facing the wind that is causing enormous waves to crash around you, you are given a sense of the power at work here. From the child long ago, who cried at the whistling sound of the wind through the telegraph wires, I am now in awe of this amazing energy. When you see the giant prop of a windmill turn on the slopes of a nearby hillside, you cannot doubt that the turbulence caused by weather patterns around the world is a force to be reckoned with. This natural energy has been accessed only minimally because of the misleading lobbying by the fossil fuel companies. Politicians around the world need to acknowledge the leadership of young people like Greta Thunberg if we are going to have any hope of saving the planet from rising sea levels.

The spiritual lesson I learned from my visit to Tvind is that as a leader I need to model how to be led. It is not necessary (in fact, preferably not) for the "leader" to know all the answers and make them available to followers. So, when the young people in Denmark formulated their curriculum, they were pointing to the skills needed to help them achieve their goals. The leadership came *cooperatively* from the group – the facilitation was provided by those who were engaged to assist. Each skill-set is vital to learning and progress.

Around that time, I read a book by Postman and Weingartner, *Teaching as a Subversive Activity*. On the list of things for a teacher *not* to do was, "never ask a question to which you yourself already know the answer". Obviously, if the teacher has all the answers, no one in the room is learning, other than the children learn that teacher knows more than they do. What is really needed is for the facilitator to *model* that learning by being a learning person himself. I have not encountered many teachers who respond eagerly to such a challenge. Yet, meaningful education will not happen without this process.

Spiritually, I do not know what's best for you. If you seek understanding, you *may* find my skill-set useful to you on your journey, or maybe not. This leads me to Ivan D Illich's work *Disabling Professions*. In this book, he reveals how the professionalising of roles gives power to leaders *and* disables followers proportionally. In the churches, over many centuries, leadership created dependence (mostly passive) on the part of members, so their practice of faith was the fulfilling of set patterns and routines. There was never the slightest suggestion that these "participants" could exercise authority and power within the organisation. Not only do the professionals restrict the spiritual experience, but they also try to control it.

In Islam, this pattern is even more clearly demonstrated, since the word "Islam" itself means "surrender" or "submission". Often this is interpreted as a slavish devotion to leadership. The behaviour of the faith community is not unlike a totalitarian system – when you look at the leadership style of the Ayatollah. However, in Indonesia, only the province of Aceh, thankfully, opted to use Sharia Law as their model of criminal justice. The national government and constitution offer a more harmonious compromise throughout the country. Indonesia is the largest Muslim democracy in the world, with a population of over 270 million people.

When Khalil Kazi and I visited Jakarta in 2007, at the behest of the UK Foreign and Commonwealth Office, the number of women wearing the burqa could be counted on the fingers of one hand. What a change from Batley, West Yorkshire, where hundreds of Muslim women can be seen wearing the niqab or burqa. All the young women in Jakarta wore the hijab (headscarf) colour-coordinated to the rest of their attire.

Although the inclusive approach to Interfaith in Indonesia did not ensure total harmony, it is worthy of recognition and appreciation. We met representatives of some religious minorities who continued to experience prejudice and violence. But the model on which it is based is dedicated to offering a sense of unity among very disparate faith traditions.

Because of the presumption of submission to the will of God or Allah, we deny ourselves choice. Perhaps we do not want to risk the consequences of our choosing? Is there a fear of making judgements, without being judgemental? Religious teaching has long trained us in passive-dependence, whereby we agonise over all the distress in the world around us. Out of fear that something will go wrong, we become paralysed from doing *any*thing.

Going back to Fox's *Original Blessing* – being human is *not* a punishment for eating fruit from the Tree of Knowledge. Having grasped that fruit, we received the lesson that when we act, there are consequences. Not *good* or *bad* consequences, just consequences – some painful, some joyful. Not making choices, not acting, means consequences – possibly some pain, possibly some joy. Otherwise, we are offered an anodyne existence – or an Anadin painkilling pill. We need to be aware that when we "take something" to relieve the pain, we are also desensitising that very part of our being which experiences joy.

In a hierarchical system based on such passive-dependent models, those who get promoted to the highest positions are mostly those who evidence the greatest compliance. So, bishops and cardinals will, more likely than not, be those whose basic psychological framework is passive-dependent. (Pierre Berton: *The Comfortable Pew*, 1965). This has created a (not so) merry-go-round, which reinforces the status quo at every level, and sidelines challenge and questions of reform. Religious institutions are not the only organisations to suffer from this condition. Check out the legal system and its arbitrary connection to justice; schooling, in relation to learning; health (sickness) service vis-à-vis well-being.

In such systems, the wider membership develops a degree of apathy towards the leadership, and eventually towards the doctrine/curriculum as well. This gives the appearance that all is well because challenge has evaporated. *But*, as Paddy Doherty wisely recognised in his work among the unemployed young people in Derry during the 1970s: "Apathy is frozen violence". When the social temperature rises, confrontation and violence become inevitable.

In church terms, instead of having dialogue between clergy and people, there is now confrontation over a range of issues. This has been identified by leaders as "unacceptable behaviour". To combat it, some churches have put in place "Codes of Conduct" to contain some of the excesses that such behaviour imposes on ill-prepared clergy. Perhaps a priest has applied a "baptism policy", which requires parents to attend church for up to 6 weeks before the ceremony. This is designed to force church attendance on people who wish only for their baby to be christened. In hospitals, a man may become abusive if an operation to save his child was unsuccessful. Or a parent might berate a teacher because her child has failed an exam.

In the church, the problem is *not* with the laity – it is systemic within the organisation. In sheer frustration, after years of being regarded as cannon fodder, people are expressing their outraged hostility at how the leadership of this voluntary organisation has undervalued them. How it has preyed on their often-meagre resources to maintain the professional power of the clergy.

I am not aware that many church leaders are trained in management, although much of their work is exactly that. Our spirituality need not be unduly influenced by the dysfunction of the religious system. However, faith communities need to get a handle on this if they hope to develop a meaningful relationship with their membership in the future.

The dissolution of "professional" clergy would do much to liberate the organisation and bring refreshing light into the grey corridors of academic religion. Speaking of "grey" – I must tell you about a Muslim lady I met while doing some research on the wearing of the burqa in northern England. This is the garment designed to impose a Muslim standard of modesty on women, which includes covering the whole body, and the face, except for the eyes.

In the end, I proposed a compromise: "Well, if a woman *does* make this choice, why does she have to wear black?" To which she quickly responded, eyeing my black shirt and jeans: "Look who's talking!" The subsequent laughter released a sense of humour, which helped to generate a more positive dialogue between parties on both sides of this debate.

Religion is too often dark and overbearing – and we all carry some responsibility for allowing that to continue. Let's have a moratorium on religious darkness – there's enough of it to be found in the rest of our daily existence. Looking at the collective karma of the church, now might be a good time to review the contents of the "Book", and edit out the dark, unsuitable material, and include some modern poetry – Dylan, perhaps?

Rainbows

The Genesis story of the flood uses a *rainbow* as the sign of a promise from the creator not to drown people again in the future. Maybe we should ask why God thought it necessary to flood the Mesopotamian region in order to punish disobedient people in the first place? We can at least agree that the rainbow motif is in itself quite a beautiful image. It is even more lovely when seen from an aeroplane, where it appears as a circle, rather than as an arc. Once you know that, you stop wasting time looking for a pot of gold at the end of it!

It is a scientific phenomenon. In the western world, we are grateful to Isaac Newton, a great Christian alchemist, for breaking white light into the visible spectrum of colour through a prism. It is quite a common occurrence when the sunlight catches raindrops at a certain angle. The playing of light on glass or clear water sometimes offers the glorious vision of this rainbow effect, which makes us go "Aaaw!" Light is the clear window that opens up into all colours. No spirituality thrives without access to light – or, indeed, darkness. It takes nothing from the delight and magic of seeing a rainbow when we know precisely how it is formed.

Children are born naïve, open-minded, fun-focussed and agog. Why do we have to "educate" that out of them? So that they can fit in with the expectations of adults? Schools are not a "gift" to children from the divine, they are mechanisms through which the professionals can ensure that the past dominates their future. Schooling is different to education. Schooling blunts curiosity in order to establish compliance and uniformity – in much the same way that religion manipulates spirituality. "Education" literally means "leading out". This suggests openness to new possibilities and contemporary expression.

Have you heard Harry Chapin's song: "Flowers are red... and you don't want to see flowers any other way than the way they always have been seen"? There, in poetic/musical form, is the impact of schooling, which erases the imagination of children. That is the process by which our spiritual essence is paused in our lives. As a child, I am at the greatest point of awareness of my being, and of the possibilities that exist within each moment. If these moments are "God-controlled" from before I was born, and school-manipulated in my childhood, then that rather undermines the whole point of education.

The net effect is that, as we grow up in our faith tradition, we are infantilised by the model we have inherited. How we learn about the faith is passed on in the form of questions and answers, which are pre-arranged. We have been given hymn images of "gentle Jesus meek and mild" and "Jesus loves me this I know – cos the bible tells me so". When we hear of an angry Jesus overturning the tables of moneychangers in the temple, we don't easily assimilate that picture. And when he calls the faith leaders "Hypocrites" and "Whited sepulchres", we must assume that he was only joking. A gentle Jesus wouldn't be so forthright – would he?

That "rainbow" of genuine emotions certainly seems to be the real person of Jesus – otherwise, he was never truly human. He was a colourful, attractive person some of the time. He got on people's nerves some of the time. He rubbed the authorities up the wrong way regularly. He made friends; and got closer to some than to others. Maybe some of his friends – possibly Judas – were jealous that he loved others more than them? Maybe he himself was jealous of some of his friends' closeness with others. In our manicured traditions, we'd have difficulty in accepting that Jesus ever needed to go for a pee. Isn't a real human Jesus so much more interesting *and* credible!

Young Laura had finished shopping with her mother in Bolton one day, and just before they got to the bus stop, it started to rain. As a church door was open nearby, they popped into the porch to keep dry. The rain looked persistent, so, since they had some time before the bus arrived, they entered the main part of the building and walked around. Passing the brightly coloured windows, Laura asked about the people who were pictured in the stained glass. Her mum read the gothic script, and said, "Those are the saints

– there's St Michael, St George, St Peter and St John. Do you like them?" Laura nodded her approval just as the sun came through the rain outside, and all the coloured windows were abloom with brightness.

Shortly afterwards, they left to catch their bus and arrived home safely. When Laura's dad returned home from work later and asked the little girl what she had been doing all day, she told him: "We went shopping and then we saw the saints, Daddy".

"The saints, Laura – who are they?"

"They are the people the light shines through," declared this child, totally unaware of the depth of her insight.

In the rainbows and windmills I have encountered, I have discovered a framework of spirituality in which I can celebrate my goodness. And I am aware that this enables me to manage my life here, now. Tomorrow may offer fresh challenges and new gifts – I hope!

CHAPTER 12

—

A Spirituality for Today

"But it's the truth, even if it didn't happen."
Chief Bromden in *One Flew over the*
Cuckoo's Nest – KEN KESEY

We have asked questions of religions that have dominated spiritual thinking in the world for centuries. They will survive our curiosity. Whether we can engineer space to develop within, alongside, or beyond their influence is our individual choice. We now know what to expect from religious teachers, so there is no longer the excuse that they misled us. We are our own leaders. My faith is mine. What beliefs I share with others may lead me into a community where I enjoy encouragement and support.

Two hallmarks of a valid spirituality are that it is authentic and alive; that it resonates with the world – people, animals, vegetation and location; that it is open to feeling the frustration of others. I want to enjoy a way of living where entitlement and privilege belong to everyone, not just to the few. I want to do something risky today, so my spirit is activated, and my heart leaps.

When we organised a parish men's group outing to climb a mountain, people thought we were crazy. We were – very crazy! We decided to head for Mt Kenya, in the hope we might reach above 16,000 feet. This is considerably lower than Mt Kilimanjaro and much less touristy, but just as demanding. The anxiety here was that two of us were old-age pensioners, albeit with plenty of experience of mountain walking. One risk is that after 12,000 feet, the possibility of altitude sickness increases significantly, although age and physical fitness have little bearing on one's susceptibility to this condition.

We spent a few days in Nairobi getting acclimatised. On the Sunday before the climb "proper" we visited the National Park and walked up to 11,000 feet. Some of us found that exercise quite challenging. Then early on Wednesday, we set out on our trek. We had a lead guide and four assistants, two of whom would cook our meals for us. We were to camp for three nights before our ascent to the peak. Nighttime temperatures were minus 4 degrees Celsius – on the Equator!

At 2 am on Saturday, the third night, we were awoken, given a warm drink and a sandwich, and began inching our way up what was a very steep face – in the dark! There were some moments of panic and a few scary losses of footing, but we persevered, mainly because, by a certain point, there was no going back. By torchlight at 6.30, and in freezing cold, wrapped up for the Arctic, we emerged onto a flat surface just below the peak. As we helped each other up onto the very top, the sun broke through the horizon to bathe us in a wonderful orange glow. We had made it. All the aches and fears dissolved into a mood of gratitude and celebration.

Ben, David, Thomas and Dick – you are all wonderful leaders. We made it up, and we made it down, *together*! The world is in awe of our humble achievement. This was an example of a giant leap for our individual, and collective, spirit. We moved way beyond our comfort zone. We realised how deeply connected we were – especially on that final morning climb to the peak. Together we went over 7,000 km away from home, and 5 km upwards to uncover new dimensions to our inner being.

There was no Sermon on the Mount. We waved our Irish flag. We took photographs. In daylight, we could now see snow around the peak. We could just about pick out the top of Kilimanjaro, some 200 km south-east. Fortunately, the return journey was not back down the steep slope, but rather more gently across some rocky terrain and easing back towards our last night at Camp Mackinder, by now exhausted, yet carried on a wave of exhilaration. The accompanying music on our adventure is in our minds, and our physical movement has a magical lightness to it. We are on a high. This is a spiritual experience. We can feel "the wind beneath our wings".

Some people discover this state by using drugs. Ancient peoples from the Americas still avail of leaves and mushrooms to heighten their awareness of another level of being. Some religious activities are accompanied using these materials. Could it be that incense used in Christian traditions bears the hallmark of such practices? Certainly, our consciousness can be affected by using certain drugs. People like John Lilly (*The Deep Self*, 1977) used his own experience to test LSD. He also experimented with an isolation tank and compared the effect of isolation and darkness to an LSD trip. Our minds can conjure up amazing imagery, apparently out of nowhere.

Quite a number of Christian ascetics, monks and saints in Britain and Ireland, as well as other places, have taken time away from their communities in isolation, often on tiny islands or in narrow caves. Beehive cells are another feature of this practice. Presumably, this was to commune with the divine, and deepen their consciousness of what is real in human existence. Some saintly writings testify to the merit of these experiences – St Patrick's "Breastplate" and "The Confession" and St Columba's "Why I Love the Oakwood of Doire".

When we look at ancient texts and we divine meaning and understanding, we do not always come up with wisdom. We need to assimilate the truths into our lives and relate them to what is real for us, so we grow to an ever-deeper understanding. Our life experience teaches us about darkness and water and wind. We are told about the stories of old. We are not given the tools to connect these pieces in a common thread; spiritual knitting needles, if you like. When we do discover the means to connect everything, or to recognise that they are already connected, then – this is our faith. The here and now is our Promised Land.

For much of my life, I have wrestled metaphorically with people who demanded *certainty* for their beliefs, as though statements of religion could parallel the empirical facts of science, or the reality of our own experience. While we were wrestling, science itself came up with a process of questioning many of its own "facts". Out of this process have emerged theories of the origins of the universe, the Earth and human life – with much research and risk attached.

Quantum physics prompts us to recognise all matter as living – that it is all interconnected at the deepest level. Much of this is beyond our academic understanding, and yet it is still truth. There's a Medic contributor to the *Private Eye* magazine (UK), who recently referred to: "the fact that science is built on error and uncertainty". The church's response to what is unknown is that it is a "mystery". Of course, there is mystery and the "Cloud of Unknowing".[8] But I do not choose to have my curiosity dismissed without exploring what is, or what might be. I am willing to build my faith on mistakes and uncertainty.

In *The Dancing Wu Li Masters*, a 1979 book by Gary Zukav, quantum physics strikes a chord with the "probabilities" of faith. This is an opportunity for science and religion to meet on a common ground of faith. It is also time for religious communities to stop avoiding the challenges and opportunities offered by an unstable world. Quantum physics is sometimes portrayed as a dance – the movement in and around probabilities. This appeals to me much more than having my questions dismissed as "mystery". There's a playfulness in the dance that allows us to be creative and destructive, to come together, and to move apart.

Many scientists today, who talk of "probabilities" rather than certainties, are exercising faith! The holding of these uncertainties as they continue their research is something which many early Christians may have done – especially around the first Easter and reports of the "empty tomb". Dare I say that genuine faith depends on such openness – being led into understanding through experience of the raw material. To receive wisdom only from the institutional avenues such as doctrine and sacred writings is inadequate and often distorted without the context of our contemporary human experience.

For long ages, our religious teaching has been fabricated and manipulated into "conspiracy". We have made assumptions about the veracity of past teachings without putting them to the test in our own time. I remember being licensed in Dublin's Christ Church Cathedral at Evensong one Sunday in July 1975. The archbishop asked several questions, including:

"Do you assent to the 39 Articles of Faith"?

I said "No".

Mr Fisher, the Diocesan Registrar, dressed in a gown and white bands, said: "We can't proceed, your Grace".

"Just a moment, Mr Fisher. Peter, the word *assent* simply means *acknowledge the existence of.*"

"Not in my dictionary, archbishop", and in a conciliatory moment I added, "... but I do assent to 17 of them."

Poor Fisher was by now dancing with horror. "We can't. We mustn't!" But the archbishop gently laid his hand upon the registrar's trembling arm, and said, "Shut up, Mr Fisher. We *will* proceed."

And so we did. No bolt of lightning struck either Mr Fisher or me. Even the archbishop escaped unscathed!

Clearly, there were reasons for holding to a set of beliefs at the time of the Reformation. But times change. In the 1970s and 80s, Rev Ian Paisley used this very "assenting" by Church of Ireland clergy to the 39 Articles (many of which are expressly against the Roman Catholic church) to challenge their ecumenical activity. So, it seemed totally inappropriate – and still does – that we should continue to "assent" to them in the face of present-day challenges. Our openly ecumenical commitments require a re-evaluation of such anachronisms.

From the relatively moderate Presbyterian church comes a tale that mirrors this Anglican experience. On a December morning in 1983, the Rev David Armstrong, Presbyterian minister of Limavady, had the temerity to walk across the street from his church to greet the Roman Catholic priest and wish him and his congregation "Happy Christmas". Over subsequent months, he was ousted by his church. Is this "moderate extremism", or is it fear? He and his wife eventually left Ireland, and David later became an Anglican priest.

Ecumenism

During my years of study in Dublin, a few of my fellow students and I made useful connections with the Jesuits in Milltown Park, and the seminarians at Maynooth. This gave an element of balance to my spiritual anguish. I found the whole protestant/Church of Ireland culture quite oppressive, and I reacted frequently in an anti-authoritarian mode.

In here, somewhere, I reconnected with the child I am and found levels of acceptance I had not felt for a long time – here, among a loose gathering of very odd young men, Catholic and Protestant, preparing for ordination in our respective churches. Some were young Catholic ordinands with girlfriends, who expected that compulsory celibacy would soon be removed. I began to sense in this connection something of divine forgiveness. This wasn't in the words of an absolution, but in the reality of a loose human community, flesh-cloaked spirit. Maybe not the historical Jesus, but divinely human!

This was not an intellectual ecumenism, rather an *experience* of connecting. It came at a time when people were seeking some sense of togetherness, some deeply shared belonging. (*Eternal Echoes* – John O'Donohue). Matthew Fox's *Deep Ecumenism* pointed out how this movement was so pervasive, historically, that it predated the efforts of the churches and superseded rational institutional approaches.

Today our re-frame-worked spirituality and ecumenism need to recognise that we are a people trusted by the divine – for, if not, how are we ever going to learn how to trust. In the past, we were not only unworthy, we were un*trust*worthy! She puts her trust in us, inviting us to put our trust in her. To be trusted by the divine is the beginning of a messianic calling to the whole people.

To regard messiahship as an individual responsibility is unhelpful. Sure, we need to exercise leadership in our own lives – leading powerful lives in the present. However, this has nothing at all to do with exercising power over other people. I am not sure I always appreciated that as a student. Our models of leadership from the past do not suit us anymore – we need to develop in order to become our own best models; appropriate to the times we live in.

The institutional language of authority and power can be replaced with enabling, collaborating, influence. To alter the words we use helps us to imagine different processes and different outcomes. Is it inconceivable to talk about a religious community as an enabling group – a place where people feel strengthened, safe and trusted? I do think it requires a quantum leap to reach that point – and maybe that is our challenge, our leap of faith.

For sure, if we insist on carrying with us all the baggage of the past – all the inherited mistranslations, misunderstandings, all the Jewish history and literature – we will not be light enough on our feet to be a "Light to the world"! That we have survived for two millennia is more credit to our risk-aversion rather than to our faith. And, as I have already prompted, faith is *inherently* risky.

The spiritual is not a "strand" on its own. It accompanies the nutrition we need for our bodies, and physical and mental exercise, as well as friendship and a sense of belonging. This process flourishes in supportive communities. It entails discipline and imaginative peregrinations. But, essentially, it is a musical *YES!* to life and everything which comes our way.

Converging relationships and friendships inevitably become divergent. Both directions of the tide are significant and valuable. They prompt soul-searching as a subjective experience, and the moment, however stimulating and revealing, is past, and the reality is assimilated, or not! How often have I invested the other with the gift of stirring my imagination, when I need only to have thanked her for being there, and celebrated my own powers of perception and wisdom.

Optimism is brought into our dualist thinking as something *future*. Most often the question is framed: "Are you optimistic about the future?". Can we be optimistic *in* the present? We have been told heaven, or hell, are *future* places – places where wrongs will be righted? And what about *now*? There's a wonderful (true) story about a Swedish immigrant in the US in the early 1900s. Joe Hill was a poet and singer and identified with the trade union movement in support of workers' rights. He was often arrested for "preaching" his Socialist message at street corners. When he saw how the Salvation Army delivered their message with no interference from the law, he wrote his political doctrine in verse, and sang it – unmolested now – to popular hymn tunes, at the very street corners where he had previously been arrested! One memorable verse which goes well to the tune of: "In the sweet by and by":

You will eat, by and by,
In that glorious land above the sky.
Work and pray, live on hay
You'll get pie in the sky when you die
Crowd: That's a lie!

This is clearly a spiritual and political cry for *now* rewards – not just the (questionable) promise of suffering in this life to enjoy glory in the next. If you get the opportunity, enjoy the film, "The Ballad of Joe Hill". Until then, you might listen to the song, "Joe Hill". There are some renditions of it on YouTube.

To achieve a sense of balance, and power, and belonging, it is vital that we develop our spiritual awareness. By doing so, we can ensure that we understand how a new, dynamic life is not in competition with other people's lives but engenders the gifts of affirmation and delight which are essential to our *collective* growth. If we stop having fun, then the whole experience reverts to an institution of dreary repetition and calling on the faith of our fathers to see us through.

For Christians, it may be helpful to revisit some of the words of Jesus and re-imagine his relatively short messianic leadership in order to get a handle on this. Who would choose to be a messiah, when you know it will end in disaster and betrayal by the people who claimed to love you most? We can explore whether he called followers to the realms of the divine (the Kingdom), or to build an institution (the Church) that would go on to dilute or reinterpret every word he uttered. Did he ever claim to be "the Son of God" any more than we are all children of the divine?

You are your own movement
The way lies within you.
You are in charge of your coming and going.
Appreciate the beauty of your moving, your growing.
You are amazing!
Be confident, in your travels,
that the Earth moves to meet you
to recognise within you
a glorious part
of her own beauty.
The world needs your strength,
your courage –
most of all, perhaps, your love.
Give freely: receive graciously.
Know, at each moment, that you are... wonderful.
Being!

ENDNOTES

8. *Cloud of Unknowing*. Written in the late fourteenth century. It suggests that the way to know God is to stop focussing on the inherited descriptions of God and dare to allow yourself to enter the realm of "unknowing". From here, you may begin to encounter the nature of the divine.

Reading Material

Reading material I found helpful for this publication, and for my life, generally:

RICHARD BACH:
- *Jonathan Livingston Seagull*
- *Illusions*
- *There's No Such Place as Far Away*

PIERRE BERTON:
- *The Comfortable Pew*

EDWARD DE BONO:
- *Rock Logic, Water Logic*

JOHN O'DONOHUE:
- *Eternal Echoes*
- *Anam Cara*

MATTHEW FOX:
- *Original Blessing*
- *One river many wells*
- *The Coming of the Cosmic Christ*

PAULO FREIRE:
- *Pedagogy of the Oppressed*

KHALIL GIBRAN:
- *The Prophet*

IVAN D ILLICH:
- *Deschooling Society*
- *Energy and Equity*
- *Limits to Medicine – Medical Nemesis*
- *Disabling Professions*
- *Tools for Conviviality*
- *Celebration of Awareness*

JOHN LILLEY:
- *The Deep Self*

POSTMAN AND WEINGARTNER:
- *Teaching as a Subversive Activity*

GARY ZUKAV:
- *The Dancing Wu Li Masters*

Acknowledgements

My sincere appreciation to all the following who had a direct hand in the production of this book, and others who have been great influencers in my life and living, past and present.

- **Paul Slack**, my artist friend, for his attention to detail, and fulsome encouragement throughout the development of this book. We first met in prison, a place that taught us many rich lessons.
- **Doug Steen**, another bohemian friend, with musical and other artistic talents, who uncovered much careless phraseology in my draft manuscript. He has cheered me with his entertaining insights into the human condition over nearly 40 years.
- **Paddy "Bogside" Doherty**, who inspired me to think outside the box, and dared me to imagine new possibilities in every situation.
- **Kate Jenkins**, who exemplifies trust like no other person I have met – and who is a well of compassion that appears never to run dry.
- **Mike Dixon**, a former prison chaplain who in retirement became a Durham County Councillor, and Vice-Chair of the Council, a tireless campaigner against injustice, and a Jazz radio host.
- **Vicky Ackroyd**, a friend who is reflective and impulsive – sometimes both at the same time – and who is prepared to go the extra mile to ensure that people are treated equally and fairly.

- **Brian Smeaton,** whose liberated leadership of himself has been a most wonderful model of wholeness and movement for me, as I have grown into being myself.
- **Joyce Byrne**, mother, teacher, leader, for whom nothing is impossible – and who treats the extraordinary as just another step along the way.
- **Kevin Dalton,** who operated as a community leader long before they had invented the role. His generous encouragement raised me up during several critical periods of my life.
- **Thomas Neale,** who lives close to the Earth, trusts his instincts and backs his hunches as he offers strength and hope in family and community – a man who shows disarming emotional intelligence.
- **Trevor Sullivan,** who thought I was somebody, and even helped me to realise it myself. He helped initiate the Irish Peace Process long before others were aware of how much it would one day be needed.
- **Hayden Foster,** a great ecumenical leader who developed into a "Group" leadership role, like no other – angrily described by one group participant as "the guy in the suit"! – and once wrote me "If you seek for Eldorado, ride, boldly ride!" (*Edgar Allan Poe*)
- **John Brown,** (The Warden) whose capacity for forgiveness was unbounded, and who created the space for others to rebel.

THANK YOU.

Note from the Author

My next book, *Butterflies and Bees*, will be published within the coming year. This book will focus on how our spirituality finds practical application in our decision making and daily living – a sort of *Applied Spirituality*.

It will look at how a Protestant teenage boy in 1960s Northern Ireland was trained in the use of guns. How his life direction was altered by fine margins in a Royal Navy eye test. How a man who could be so positive and clear in public matters could be so disordered in his personal life and his relationships.

If you want to be kept informed, to pass on comments, or to receive updated information, please go and register on the website **www.fallhappy.com** or email me at **peterstewarttarleton@gmail.com**

PETER TARLETON STEWART